The
Essential
Thai
Cookbook

The Essential Thai Cookbook

Vatcharin Bhumichitr

CLARKSON N. POTTER, INC./PUBLISHERS, NEW YORK

For My Father, Chun Bhumichitr

Copyright © 1994 by Vatcharin Bhumichitr
Location Photographs Copyright © 1994 by John Everingham
Recipe and ingredients photographs copyright © by Roger Stowell

Published by Clarkson N. Potter, Inc. Publishers, 201 East 50th Street, New York, New York 10022. Member of the Crown Publishing Group.

Random House, Inc. New York, Toronto, London, Sydney, Auckland
Originally published in Great Britain by Pavilion Books Limited in 1994

CLARKSON N. POTTER, POTTER, and colophon are trademarks of Clarkson N. Potter, Inc.

Manufactured in Italy

Design by Andrew Barron & Collis Clements Associates

Library of Congress Cataloging-in-Publication Data

Vatcharin Bhumichitr.
   The essential Thai cookbook / Vatcharin Bhumichitr. —
1st American ed.
     p.   cm.
   Includes index.
   1. Cookery. Thai.   I. Title.
TX724.5. T5V36   1994
641.59593—dc20   94-6395
                                       CIP

ISBN 0-517-59630-X

10 9 8 7 6 5 4 3 2 1

First American Edition

◀◀
A congregation of seated Buddhas watches over the temple of Wat Pai Rong Wua near Supanburi, central Thailand.

CONTENTS

INTRODUCTION
A BUFFALO AT DAWN

It sometimes seems that lemon grass has become the world's most popular ingredient. You find it in all manner of dishes, cooked by all sorts of chefs, and it even turns up in quite modest supermarkets in towns where you would least expect to find this plant that was, until recently, little known outside Asia.

And it's not just lemon grass – kaffir lime, galangal and coriander all have a role in Western cooking as a result of the rapid growth in the popularity of Thai restaurants in Europe and North America. Most large cities in the West now have some sort of shop that specializes in these formerly 'exotic' ingredients. It will most probably be Chinese or Indian, but some cities also have Thai food shops, selling specifically Thai varieties. Most are a combination of old-style open market and modern pre-packaged supermarket, with fresh products sold loose and a few items such as beancurd and noodles being offered in wrapped portions. Although many Western cooks are now trying Asian recipes, these foodstuffs can still seem strange and the stores that sell them remain rather forbidding. Many ingredients are difficult to identify and it is hard to know which to choose, let alone how to prepare and preserve them once you get home.

Part of the problem lies in the shops which are often selling packaged goods that the shopkeepers themselves barely understand. This problem is not confined to Europe and North America. I only have to take a two minute walk from my family home in the centre of Bangkok to see how the selling of food, like everything else in Thailand, has been transformed by the rapid economic growth of the past twenty years. In a little *soi* or narrow lane running off the main road near our house is the old market where my mother used to shop when I was a child. This large wooden hall with its darkened beams still offers all the bounty of the Thai countryside: beansprouts and mangoes, piles of fresh smelling lemon grass, mountains of cabbages and aubergines/eggplants, baskets heaped with vivid scarlet chilies, tubs filled with pungent deep purple shrimp paste or ochre bamboo shoots, rank upon rank of pickling jars with their intriguing contents – all the heady sights and smells of Asia. Now, by one of those twists of fate, this old weather-beaten structure has a new neighbour, right opposite – a mammoth concrete skyscraper soaring to the heavens, with a brand new department store at its base containing a modern supermarket. Here, in air-conditioned comfort, the shopper can wheel a trolley and select neat packages of washed and ready-peeled green mango, carefully portioned boxes of sweet basil, and coconut milk in cans. There are even ready-to-cook meals, all the ingredients chopped and measured and carefully set out under a transparent

▶
Succulent crab from the
Gulf of Thailand.

wrapper. Go to the wooden market and you will see that the old know how to choose, while in the supermarket the young know only how to buy.

Having lived in London for over eighteen years, I have seen this problem transferred to the West. When I first arrived, oriental ingredients were virtually unknown. They arrived 'loose', dumped in a few Chinese shops, only for those who already knew about them. But now that they are sold in ordinary supermarkets, the situation is hardly any better, for neither outlet tells the newcomer anything about the ingredient itself and most cookbooks assume a basic knowledge that few have.

This book sets out to remedy that situation. I have taken the principal ingredients of Thai cooking and broken them down into related groups, with each one set out in as clear a manner as possible, so that you can see what it looks like and learn how to select the best and then how to use and keep it for as long as possible. Each ingredient is followed by a selection of recipes that show the various ways the ingredient can be used. I hope this will be helpful, both to those who are trying Thai cooking for the first time, as well as anyone who has already made a start but would like to know more about the basic elements that underpin our cuisine.

At the same time I have divided the book into four sections, based on the main regions of Thailand, in order to set these ingredients in a living context. I've done this in the form of four journeys that I made and which you might like to make too. It's not intended to be a guide book, but more a personal exploration of some of the more unusual byways of my homeland, a sort of *cook's tour* with a small c.

It is always a great mistake to think of food as something that simply turns up in a shop; despite the clever packaging, we should never forget that as cooks, we are simply one more link in a long chain that reaches back to the fields and farms and those who work in them. Too many city dwellers only glimpse this other world as they flash past in their cars – a buffalo being led through the paddies at dawn, a fisherman casting his gauzy net over a glistening river, a group of distant figures bending to tend rice in a flooded field. Yet we should never allow ourselves to be too alienated from what is, after all, the source of our own well-being. Every time we go to market and then cook and share our food, we should feel at one with those who provided it and thus gave us the wherewithall to live. That, ultimately, is the reason for this book.

BEFORE YOU BEGIN

EQUIPMENT

You will need the following:

1 A chopping board and a range of sharp kitchen knives in varying sizes. A Chinese chopping 'axe', or cleaver, would prove very useful.

2 A wok or a large frying pan or skillet, with a long-handled wooden spoon or spatula.

3 A saucepan with a tight-fitting lid for cooking rice, or, best of all, an electric rice steamer.

4 A mortar and pestle.

5 A steamer. You could use Chinese bamboo steamers or improvise with a saucepan, using an upturned heatproof bowl to support a plate above the boiling water in the pan.

6 A coarse mesh, long-handled sieve or strainer for deep frying or dipping noodles, and slotted spoon for removing ingredients from hot oil.

TECHNIQUES

Most of the hard work involved in making Thai food comes at the preliminary stages when the ingredients are cut and chopped – the actual cooking is usually done quite quickly. There are various ways in which an ingredient can be prepared and the following are the main expressions used in this book:

finely chopped, roughly chopped, sliced, diced, slivered lengthways, slivered into fine matchsticks, cut into wedges, ovals and rounds. Also, see the picture below.

The commonest instruction is to 'stir-fry'. This means tossing the ingredients into a wok and stirring and turning them rapidly over high heat, frying them just enough so that the hardest ingredient is cooked no more than *al dente*, then turning them on to a serving dish. Be bold and quick. *Never* over-cook!

◄
From left to right:
Top row: Finely sliced; finely chopped; slivered into matchsticks.

Second row: Cut into rounds: finely sliced diagonally into ovals: rolled into a cigarette and finely slivered.

Third row: Cut into wedges.

Bottom row: Cut into 2 in/5 cm lengths, then halved and quartered; cut into small cubes.

WEIGHTS & MEASURES

Except for one-dish meals, such as some rice and noodle dishes, the recipes given here are for quite small portions on the assumption that you will be serving three or four or even five dishes together in the Thai style.

Dry Measures

Small amounts are given in teaspoons and tablespoons, expressed as tsp and tbsp. These are equivalent to metric spoon measures: 1 tsp = 5 ml, 1 tbsp = 15 ml. Larger amounts are given in ounces or pounds followed by a metric equivalent. Thus: 1 oz/30 g, 1 lb/480 g. In cases where an American cook would measure the ingredient by volume, the equivalent cup measure is added. Thus: 8 oz/240 g/1¼ cups sticky rice.

Liquid Measures

UK and US pints and quarts are different and here I have given fluid ounces or Imperial measures, followed by a metric equivalent, followed by US cups. Thus: 4 fl oz/120 ml/ ½ cup, 8 fl oz/240 ml/1 cup, 1 pint/600 ml/ 2½ cups. Note that any pints referred to are Imperial pints (20 fl oz) and not American pints (16 fl oz).

Linear Measures

These are given first in inches, feet, etc. followed by the metric equivalent. Thus: ¼ inch/5 mm, ½ inch/1.25 cm, 1 inch/2.5 cm.

Egg Sizes

Where a recipe calls for eggs, these are size-3 eggs (US large eggs). Any other egg sizes required are specified.

▲
In Ang Sila, on the coast just south-east of Bangkok, the young stone carver Thanong-Sa works on one of the mortars for which the little village is famous. (Photograph by the author.)

THE THAI MEAL

Apart from a quick snack, perhaps fried rice or a dish of noodles, no Thai would willingly eat alone. Meals are shared, and consist of a number of dishes, served with rice, into which the diners dip with their spoons, taking as much as they like of each in turn, returning to a particular dish when they feel inclined. That is why the recipes in this book are for quite small quantities, the assumption being that you will be preparing three, four or even five dishes to make up a meal for perhaps three to four diners.

A separate course to open the meal – hors-d'œuvre – was not part of Thai traditional dining. However, it was not unusual for certain, rather spicy dishes, to be prepared slightly in advance of the main meal, and served as an accompaniment to drinks before the actual dinner began. Nowadays, with the spread of European modes of entertaining, these 'starters' are sometimes served as a first course.

Ideally, the main meal should consist of a number of small dishes which should balance each other. There are many ways to combine different types of recipes in a meal, but one menu might be: a curry, a fried dish, a steamed dish, a *yam* spicy salad or a spicy dip, and a soup (this is not a separate course in Thai dining but is dipped into as with the other dishes). There is always rice – plain boiled white rice in most of the country and steamed sticky rice in the north. If it is the more usual plain boiled rice, then a little heap is placed on each diner's plate, after which everyone dips into the bowls to take what they wish to their plates. Forks and spoons are the preferred implements – chopsticks and bowls are only used for noodles. Drink what you like best – older Thai men drink beer, whisky or brandy, but younger Thais of both sexes are turning to wine, which goes well with anything save the hottest dishes.

The main meal would normally be followed by a selection of Thai fruits. On grander occasions it is usual to offer fruit along with a solid dessert, (a *kanom* or cake) and a liquid dessert (a sort of dessert soup).

To give you some idea of how to combine dishes for a meal, here is one selection:

Hors-D'Œuvre
H Fish Cakes with Kaffir Lime Leaf *Tod Man Pla* (page 124)

Main Course
S Hot and Sour Soup with Prawns and Lemon Grass *Tom Yam Gung* (page 133)
C Mussaman Curry *Gaeng Mussaman* (page 92)
F Fried Fish with Crispy Garlic *Pla Tod Kratiam Krop* (page 72)
T Stuffed Hot Peppers *Prik Sod Sy* (page 81)
Y Hot and Sour Pomelo Salad *Yam Som Oh* (page 176)

Desserts
Fruit
K Waterchestnuts with Bandan Leaf and Coconut Cream *Tako Hel* (page 181)
L Bananas in Coconut Milk *Kluay Bua Chee* (page 176)

Each recipe in this book is marked with a letter to tell you which part of a meal it is, so that you can make your own selections.

O One-dish meals, rice or noodles
H Hors-d'œuvres: dishes that can be used as first courses or as snacks to go with drinks. (They can also be served as part of the main meal if you wish.)
S Soups
C Curries
F Fried, grilled, roasted or stewed dishes
D Spicy dips
T Steamed dishes
Y *Yam*: hot and sour salads
K *Kanom* or solid desserts
L Liquid desserts
V Vegetarian: this letter will follow one of the others when the dish is vegetarian, so that those wishing to have meat-free meals can

STOCK

make combinations with ease. (As the desserts are automatically meat-free they are not marked with a **V**.)

The following is a very copious vegetarian meal to show how the system can be used:
HV Spicy Sweetcorn Cakes *Tod Man Khao Pohd* (page 29)
HV Grilled Mushrooms with Garlic and Chili Sauce *Het Hom Yang* (page 69)

followed by:
SV Hot and Sour Vermicelli Soup *Rang Nok Tiam* (page 120)
CV Vegetable Curry *Gaeng Pa Jay* (page 165)
DV Chiang Mai Spicy Dip *Nam Prik Num* (page 81)
FV Fried Curried Aubergine with Yellow Bean Sauce *Pad Pet Makua Tow Jeow* (page 44)
TV Steamed Mushroom Curry with Sweet Basil *Muk Het* (page 117)
YV Hot and Sour Bamboo Salad *Sup Normai* (page 121)

Many of the recipes in this book call for stock to be used. I always have a stock pot on the go in my restaurant, but I appreciate that in the modern home this may be difficult to maintain, as the liquid must be thoroughly boiled every day and kept in constant use. As a result most people will have to rely on stock or bouillon cubes or canned stock or broth, unless they can buy fresh stock in cartons. However, if you are planning to do a lot of cooking and would like the more authentic taste of real stock, then the task is fairly easy.

For *meat stocks* – beef, chicken etc. – simply cover the bones or carcasses with water, bring to the boil and simmer for 2 hours, skimming from time to time as necessary. Use no herbs or spices. Add more bones or carcasses as they appear. Remember that you must boil up the stock every day or else pour it into plastic containers and freeze.

For *vegetable stock* combine 1 quartered onion, 2 roughly chopped carrots, 2 roughly chopped celery stalks, 3–4 coriander roots and 1 teaspoon of black peppercorns in the pot. Most hard vegetables will do, but avoid highly flavoured, highly coloured vegetables such as beetroot/beets. Cover with cold water and bring to the boil. Continue boiling until the liquid is reduced by about a fifth.

1

THE
HEART OF
THE
KINGDOM

◆

BANGKOK,
THE
CENTRAL PLAINS
AND THE
GULF COAST

16

Every morning before dawn, an old lady, dressed in a simple *panung,* a wrap-around cloth skirt, and a plain cotton blouse, the standard habit of the poor in Thailand, sets up her stall at the end of my family's *soi* in Bangkok and begins to cook her speciality, Issan chicken. By 7 a.m., the sun has risen and several golden brown chicken breasts, spread on bamboo skewers, are gently sizzling on her charcoal stove. She, meanwhile, is sitting by the roadside before a heavy stone mortar in which she is pounding the shredded green papaya, nuts, chilies and tomatoes for the spicy *Som Tam* salad that accompanies the grilled meat. By this time the diminutive figure is completely swamped by the Bangkok traffic, a solid mass of cars heading towards the Silom Road business district, bumper to bumper, pouring out the pollution that envelops the entire downtown area in a yellow fog.

It is impossible to exaggerate the contradictions of life in a city that has leapt from the tranquil Middle Ages to the twenty-first century practically overnight. Once famed as the Venice of the East, a place of charming wooden houses built along the *klongs,* or canals, that ran into the mighty Chao Phraya River, Bangkok has become a futuristic megalopolis – with no period of adaptation in between. As the foodsellers by the busy roadside show, the two worlds exist in an odd harmony. I have a friend, a successful lawyer, who got so fed up with the three hour journey to and from his office, with frequent, unexplained delays adding to the nightmare, that he now has himself driven to work in a camper van, with a bed and a television, so that he can lie back at his ease watching the latest video releases. In modern Bangkok even the poor have portable telephones – how else could they keep in touch with family and friends in the universal traffic jam?

At least there is no problem about food, which is the one thing in Thailand that still links the gentle past to this crazy future. If your car is stuck and you are hungry, you only have to open the door to find a line of cooks along the pavement, ready to sell you duck noodle soup, fried rice with pork and beansprouts, tasty little beef balls with a sweet and hot sauce, or *Pahd Thai* noodles with dried shrimps. The list is endless, as are the cooks who, like the lady with her Issan chicken, flood into the capital, bringing their regional dishes with them, hoping to make a living in *Krung Thep,* the City of Angels, our name for the place the world knows as Bangkok.

Everyone who comes to Thailand has to visit Bangkok, and is usually thrilled with the regular tourist sites – the Grand Palace, the Temple of the Dawn, the Emerald Buddha, the colourful march past

◄◄
On the edge of Lumpini park, the statue of King Rama VI watches over the new Bangkok.

of the Royal Guard, the spectacular burst of fireworks over the city on the King's birthday. Of course, what they are seeing is the city as it was, built along the river where all human activity was once concentrated. The rivers of Thailand have been central to its history and culture, providing water for the paddy fields and fish for the table, and acting as both highways and defensive barriers. Traditionally, many Thai people have led an almost amphibious existence – as much in the water as out of it. Four of the principle northern rivers – the Ping, Wang, Yam and Nan – merge just above the city of Nakhon Sawan to form the single great Chao Phraya River that crosses the broad emerald plains of rice, on its way south to the Gulf of Thailand. These central plains, along with the coastal strip to the west and east of the Chao Phraya's estuary, make up the heart of the nation, a great triangle that has the ruined former capital of Ayuthaya as its apex, and the cities of Petchaburi and Chantaburi as its western and eastern points, with the modern capital Bangkok, just over 200 years old, between them, near the river's mouth.

For the tourists, it is almost as if old Siam still exists. Much of what they see stands on the Chao Phraya's banks. They will be taken to see the floating market, a colourful huddle of narrow boats, low in the water with the heavy loads of vegetables, herbs and fruit, each rowed by a woman in a wide-brimmed hat, keen for the visitors to see how good her produce is. Some boats are floating kitchens with noodle steamers on board, so that even by or on the river, you are never far from a quick snack.

Modern Bangkok has turned its back on the river, filling in the *klongs* to make highways for yet more traffic jams, and spreading north into what were once untouched rice fields, or skywards with ever higher tower blocks. Having lived abroad for much of my adult life, I used to spend quite a lot of time moaning about the appalling changes at home, and praying that it would all stop and that things would be as they once were. On my last visit to Bangkok I suddenly realized that it was pointless to go on complaining. I even read a newspaper article about a campaign being set up to save what remains of the old city – a sure sign that it is too late. In fact I have now accepted that the old Bangkok is irretrievably lost and that something, not yet fully formed, is struggling to take its place. I saw it first from a spot not far from my family home, on the edge of Lumpini Park, looking out towards the business district, where sheer white towers now glisten in the sunlight, a vision of tomorrow both exciting and disturbing. Having been born in a modest Third World country, this awesome evidence of the economic boom, which has

transformed Thailand into a thrusting partner in the economic miracle of the Pacific Rim, is quite breathtaking.

It is poignant that just at that point, on the edge of the park, where this vision of the future is most clear, there still stands the massive bronze statue honouring King Rama VI, the last ruler of Thailand to try to create a masterplan for his capital. This king wanted to build a new, rational city, with broad avenues and open spaces, in the area around what is now the park. He even had a great model made to show how his dream might one day look and one can still see some faded black and white photographs of it in the Library Bar of the nearby Dhusit Thani Hotel. These are so intriguing that one cannot help but feel sorry that the model itself was not preserved – the nearby figures in the photographs look like giants striding round Lilliput. Our family name 'Bhumichitr' means 'map-maker', and one of these figures could well be my grandfather who was responsible for drawing up the plans for the new city.

Unfortunately, King Rama VI died in 1925, after a fifteen-year-reign, and the plan died with him. The absolute monarchy was abolished under the next king, and successive governments, whether military or democratic, have let development take place on a purely haphazard basis – hence the traffic, the pollution, and the amazing sprawl as the city gets ever bigger. All that remains of King Rama's dream is the park itself, laid out by my grandfather along the lines of the English public gardens that the king had admired when, as Crown Prince, he had been a schoolboy at Eton.

There are, however, many ways in which the view of the city offered to the tourist is still a living reality, for despite the skyscrapers and the flyover expressways and all the other symbols of modernity, Bangkok is still fed by the great river. Rice is still the single most important element in Thai life, and the swollen hump-backed barges that meander in convoys down the Chao Phraya to the port at Klong Toey are as important to the nation as all the office-workers and designers and television personalities who seem to dominate modern life. Rice, and noodles made from rice flour, are the two staples of the Thai diet.

◀
December fifth, fireworks over the Dusit Prasad Throne Hall, Bangkok, in honour of the King's birthday.

▶
The spectacular Royal Guard troop the colour on the King's birthday.

If one continues along the river, out past Klong Toey to its
estuary on the gulf, one can find the other basic ingredients essential
to Thai cooking: fish sauce, dried shrimps and dried shrimp paste. If
you can't go by boat, then a short car journey, 60 kilometres east of
the capital, will bring you to the fishing village of Ang Sila. When I
was young I used to go on sketching trips with my fellow art
students to what was then a sleepy little hamlet. Some of the old
atmosphere remains, though the occasional concrete shop-house –
with its trading area at ground level and accommodation above – has
crept in amongst the traditional wooden stilt houses built out over
the sea. But a visit is still worth the effort as Ang Sila plays a crucial
role in Thai cookery – you *hear* it as soon as you approach the town –
the bell-like ring of hammer against stone! As you drive in, you begin
to pass roadside displays of statuary: Buddhas and lions and garden
ornaments, but mostly rack upon rack of hollowed-out stone mortars,
hefty things for really serious cooks. They used to be carved from the
sand coloured rock found in the sea nearby, but today that is a rarity.
One of the local sculptors, Thanong-Sa, explained to me that they
now have to import a blue-grey granite from the local hills. Thanong-
Sa was twenty-three when I talked to him, but he said that he had
been carving since the age of thirteen, taught by his mother, and that
his hands were now as hard as the tough rock he has to work with.

     A short walk from Thanong-Sa's workshop, I came upon a store
at the centre of the Ang Sila market, where I noticed some light
coloured bottles of fish sauce, which I knew must be home-made.
Fish sauce is the basic flavouring for Thai food and many commercial
brands are quite dark and bitter. The best is whisky coloured and has
a light refreshing taste. It turned out that the few bottles I had seen
were produced by the shop's owner, Mrs Arom, and they were
surplus to her own needs. She also sells other key flavourings such as
tiny dried shrimps and pungent shrimp paste, but it was her fish
sauce that interested me. This sauce is made all along the coast,
especially in the town of Rayong where many of the manufacturers
are based, but this sort of light home-made variety is hard to find.

     After we had spoken for a while, Mrs Arom showed me to her
house at the back of the shop, which was surrounded by thirty or so
large Ali Baba jars, or *tum* as we call them, in which the pounded fish
and salt are left to ferment and liquefy. She explained that she only
uses a particular tiny fish, *gaa tak*, which swarms in this part of the
Gulf, and that it has to have been caught that day – she never uses
even a day-old-catch. After a year in a *tum*, the fermented liquid is
strained through muslin or cheesecloth into bottles and is then ready

for use. To the visitor, the fishy aroma from all those jars may seem a trifle overpowering, but Mrs Arom said she liked the rich sea-smell with its promise of good things to come. She usually manages to get two lots of liquid per *tum* – the first will be fresh and mild, the second darker and saltier. I was in luck because the bottles I had seen were a first pressing, light and tangy, and a good reminder of a pleasant day by the sea when I got back to Bangkok that night.

I had a final reminder of the continuing importance of the river on my most recent trip home, when I was invited to visit the Oriental Hotel's riverside Thai restaurant, the Rim Nam. I usually avoid tourist restaurants, being quite happy to eat in scruffy backstreet cafés where you find authentic Thai cooking, but Kuhn Narumol Jotivej, a senior manager at this hotel, had visited my restaurant in London and wanted to talk to me. It seems that she had been surprised to find *farangs* (foreigners) happily eating real Thai food and not the sort of doctored stuff usually prepared for visitors. On her return to Bangkok, she told her chefs to make the food as they would like to eat it, and now she wanted me to come and test the results. Having taken the little boat across from the hotel to the Thonburi side of the river, we sat on a wide terrace eating *Tod Man Pla*, chewy deep-fried fish cakes served with a fresh pickle, and *Gaeng Keow Wan*, a green curry, among the many delicious things she insisted I try.

From our vantage point it was clear that the life of the river goes on much as it always has, with the same extraordinary contradictions. You can sit in the Rim Nam being served with great finesse by waitresses wearing traditional Thai dress, only in their case the wrap-around skirt and fitted blouse are made of the finest Thai silk. As you watch, a huge rice barge glides past, deep in the water, bound for Klong Tuey, and one can see the family that lives on board, husband in his breach-clout, his wife in her faded cotton *panung*, tiny children naked, gathered around the glowing charcoal brazier eating their evening meal. The nice thing about Thailand is that despite the differences – the world of fine silk and that of cheap cotton – it is possible that the boat family was enjoying food every bit as delicious as I was. In a land as bountiful, agriculturally, as Thailand, good food is essentially democratic.

One thing that was intriguing about that river view was the number of new buildings going up along its banks – apartment blocks and condominiums – a sign, perhaps, that the citizens of Bangkok are about to return to their roots and start living near water again.

RICE
KHAO

Over half the world's population survives on rice, and its place at the heart of Thai history and culture is sacrosanct. Low in calories, yet capable of supplying nearly 80 per cent of the body's energy requirements, bland enough to make the perfect accompaniment to a wide range of dishes, yet delicious enough to be eaten in quantity, this small white grain is almost the perfect foodstuff.

There are some eleven varieties of rice grown around the planet but only two are used regularly in Thai cuisine. I have totally ignored fast food products such as boil-in-the-bag rice or microwave versions – if you wish to cook Thai food then use Thai rice. It is quite simply the best, and we export enough of it for it to be easily available. Also, as will become clear, cooking Thai rice perfectly is the easiest thing imaginable – so forget short cuts. They are never worth it!

Thai Fragrant Rice
This is the name under which Thai rice is sold abroad. It is a long-grain, jasmin-scented rice and is of the highest quality. It is served boiled or steamed and can be reheated in a variety of ways, most often fried. The grains can be dry-fried in a wok or frying pan; this is sometimes known as grilled rice (*Khao Kua*) and is used to give a crunchy texture and a nutty, slightly burnt flavour to a dish (see recipe page 24).

Long-grain rice is also used for making rice vinegars. These vary from light to the more strongly flavoured, older, dark red varieties. If you are buying Chinese rice vinegars, which are the easiest to find, you should try to avoid those that contain monosodium glutamate or other seasonings. Unless otherwise specified, when I refer to rice vinegar in this book I mean the lighter variety rather than the darker, aged vinegars.

Overleaf is the classic recipe for plain boiled rice.

▲
Morning glory/Water spinach; whole green peppercorns; betel leaves (see p 137).

▶
Rice (*Khao*)
Against a background of uncooked Thai Fragrant Rice:
Top left: Uncooked sticky or glutinous rice (*Khao Niew*).
Top right: Cooked sticky or glutinous rice (*Khao Niew*).
Middle left: Dry fried rice (*Khao Kua*).
Middle right: Powdered dry fried rice (*Khao Kua*).
Bottom left: Cooked Thai fragrant rice (*Khao Suay*).
Bottom right: Crispy rice (*Khao Tang*), plain and deep fried.

Boiled Rice *Khao Suay*

1 lb/480 g/2½ cups Thai fragrant rice

1 pint/600 ml/2½ cups water

An experienced Thai cook varies the water according to the age and thus the dryness of the rice; the above is a reasonable average ratio.

Rinse the rice thoroughly at least three times in cold water, until the water runs clear. Put the rice in a heavy saucepan and add the measured water. Cover and quickly bring to the boil. Uncover and cook, stirring vigorously, until the water level is below that of the rice whose surface will begin to look dry. Turn the heat down as low as possible, cover the pan again (put a layer of foil under the lid, if necessary, to ensure a tight fit) and steam for 20 minutes.

The good news is that none of this is really necessary. Buy a rice-steamer: they are cheap, super-efficient, and make and keep perfect rice with absolutely no fuss or bother.

Crispy Rice *Khao Tang*

If, when boiling rice, an accident occurs and you are left with rice sticking to the bottom of the pan, do not worry as nothing is wasted in Thai cooking.

First soak the pan in cold water and then lift away the sheet of rice and dry it. Break it into 3 or 4 pieces. Heat a pan of oil for deep frying. Fry the rice pieces until they are golden brown and crisp. Drain on paper towels.

Sticky or Glutinous Rice *Khao Niew*

This is a broad, short-grain rice, mostly white although sometimes brown or even black. As its name implies, it is the opposite of light and fluffy, being thick and almost porridgy. It is the staple of Northern Thailand where during a meal it is plucked with the fingers, rolled into a ball and used to scoop up the other food. Sticky rice is also used throughout Thailand to make sweets, and it is milled into rice flour which is bought ready-ground.

Sticky rice cannot be cooked in an electric rice-steamer and needs to be soaked before cooking.

Steamed Sticky Rice *Khao Niew*

1 lb/480 g/2¼ cups glutinous or sticky rice

Soak the rice in water to cover for at least 3 hours, or overnight if possible. Drain and rinse thoroughly.

Line the perforated part of a steamer with a double thickness of muslin or cheesecloth and turn the rice into it. Heat water in the bottom of the steamer to boiling and steam the rice over a moderate heat for 30 minutes.

Both plain boiled rice and steamed sticky rice are basic accompaniments to nearly all the dishes in this book, so the recipes given in this section are dishes that use the rice as an ingredient rather than just a side dish.

Dry Fried Rice *Khao Kua*

Put the required amount of uncooked rice grains into a dry wok or frying pan, over a high heat. Keep shaking the pan so that the grains do not burn. Keep 'frying' until the grains are golden brown. Remove. If required, pound in a mortar, but do not reduce to a powder as the rough texture of the broken rice is important. The same method can be used for sesame seeds.

RICE SOUP (O)
KHAO TOM MOO

This is a very soothing dish, commonly eaten both for breakfast and as a mild meal for those who aren't feeling well. It is also sometimes heated up as a late supper. Rice soup is never served as part of an ordinary meal but is always eaten on its own.

2 tbsp vegetable oil
2 garlic cloves, finely chopped
16 fl oz/500 ml/2 cups chicken stock
1 tsp preserved vegetable/*tang chi* (see page 94)
1 tbsp light soy sauce
¼ tsp ground white pepper
1 tbsp fish sauce
2 oz/60 g minced/ground pork
8 oz/240 g/1¼ cup boiled fragrant rice
fresh coriander leaves/cilantro, to garnish

In a wok or frying pan, heat the oil and fry the garlic until golden brown. Remove from the heat and set aside.

In a saucepan, heat the stock with the preserved vegetable. Add the soy sauce, pepper and fish sauce. Bring to simmering point. Holding the pork loosely in one hand, pull off small pieces with the other hand and drop into the stock. When all has been added, cook for 1 minute. Add the cooked rice and stir thoroughly. Cook for a further 4–5 minutes or until the rice is heated through and soft. The soup should be quite thick.

Ladle into individual bowls. Add 1 teaspoon of the garlic and oil mixture to each and garnish with coriander leaves.

VEGETARIAN FRIED RICE (OV)
KHAO PAD MANG SA VIRAD

The most nourishing part of this dish is the beans, and I have left the choice of beans to the cook. The only thing to remember is that you should try to use a mixture – say red kidney beans and borlotti beans – to add a dash of colour. If the beans are dried, you should soak and cook them first; if canned, drain and rinse thoroughly before adding to the stir-fry.

2 tbsp vegetable oil
2 garlic cloves, finely chopped
6 tbsp mixed cooked beans
2 tbsp diced carrots
2 tbsp diced tomato
2 tbsp diced pineapple
2 tbsp light soy sauce
1 tsp sugar
½ tsp ground white pepper
8 oz/240 g/1 cup boiled fragrant rice
fresh coriander leaves/cilantro, to garnish

In a wok or frying pan, heat the oil and fry the garlic until golden brown. Stirring constantly, add each ingredient in turn, stirring well between each addition, until the rice has been added. Stir thoroughly, until the rice is heated through, then turn on to a serving dish and garnish with coriander leaves.

CURRIED RICE AND CHICKEN (O)
KHAO MOK GAI

1 medium-size chicken, weighing about 3–3½ lb/1.35–1.6 kg
4 tbsp vegetable oil
4 tbsp finely chopped garlic
1 lb/480 g/2¾ cups uncooked fragrant rice, rinsed and strained
1 tsp curry powder
2 tsp salt
16 fl oz/500 ml/2 cups chicken stock

Halve the chicken with a cleaver, then chop each half into three roughly equal pieces and set aside. In a wok or frying pan, heat the oil and fry the garlic until golden brown. Add the rice and stir well, then add the curry powder and salt and stir quickly to mix. Add the chicken pieces and stir well, then transfer the mixture to an electric rice-steamer and add the stock. Cover and cook for 20 minutes. Alternatively, put the mixture in a heatproof bowl, place in the top part of a steamer over boiling water and steam for 30 minutes. Serve with the following fresh pickle.

FRESH PICKLE (D)
ADJAHD

This makes enough for one person so you will need to multiply the quantities by the number of diners

4 tbsp rice vinegar
2 tsp sugar
½ tsp salt
3 inch/7.5 cm piece of English cucumber
2 small shallots, finely chopped
2-3 small fresh red chilies, thinly sliced

Stir the vinegar, sugar and salt together until the sugar has dissolved. Halve and then quarter the cucumber lengthways; cut across into very thin slices. Add to the liquid, along with the chopped shallots and chilies. Serve in a small bowl.

COCONUT RICE (O)
KHAO MAN GRAT TI

This is a way of adding extra interest to ordinary rice and goes well with very spicy dishes such as *yam* salads and curries. In Thailand I would make this with fresh coconut but as these are sometimes hard to obtain in the West I have adapted the recipe so that you can use canned coconut cream.

2 tbsp vegetable oil
2 garlic cloves, chopped
8 oz/240 g/1 cup cooked fragrant rice
4 tbsp coconut cream (page 178)
½ tsp salt

In a wok or frying pan, heat the oil and fry the garlic until golden brown. Add the rice and stir well until heated through. Add the coconut cream and mix well. Season with salt and serve.

CRISPY RICE WITH PORK, PRAWN/SHRIMP AND COCONUT SAUCE (H)
KHAO TANG NAA TANG

Soak, remove, break into 3 or 4 pieces and dry the rice stuck at the bottom of a pan. Heat oil and deep fry the rice pieces until they are golden brown and crispy. Drain and set aside.

The sauce:
2 garlic cloves, roughly chopped
1 tsp coriander root
1 tsp black peppercorns
4 oz/120 g minced/ground pork
2 oz/60 g minced/ground raw prawns/shrimp
2 tbsp vegetable oil
2 shallots, finely chopped
8 fl oz/240 ml/1 cup coconut milk (page 178)
1 tbsp fish sauce
1 tbsp light soy sauce
1 tbsp tamarind water (page 142)
1 tsp sugar
2 tbsp ground roasted peanuts
1 large fresh red chilli, slivered lengthways
fresh coriander leaves/cilantro, to garnish

In a mortar, pound the garlic, coriander root and peppercorns together to form a paste. Set aside.

In a bowl, mix the pork and prawns together. In a large pan, heat the oil and stir in the garlic paste. Add the mixed pork and prawns and stir well. Stirring constantly, add each of the remaining ingredients in turn down to the chili.

Turn on to a plate, garnish with coriander leaves and serve with the deep-fried rice pieces.

▲
Winnowing rice near Chiang Mai.

SPICY BEEF WITH GALANGAL AND DRY-FRIED RICE (H)
NAM TOK

8 oz/240 g piece of tender boneless beef
4 tbsp beef stock
2 tbsp fish sauce
4 tbsp lemon juice
1 tsp sugar
2 tsp finely chopped galangal
1 tsp chili powder
2 spring onions/scallions, finely chopped
2 shallots, finely chopped
1 tbsp dry-fried rice, coarsely pounded
fresh coriander leaves/cilantro, to garnish

Preheat the grill/broiler.

Very briefly grill/broil both sides of the piece of beef until it just begins to brown. On a plate, thinly slice the beef while retaining any juices. Put the sliced beef and its juices into a saucepan with the stock and heat, adding each of the remaining ingredients in turn, down to the chili powder, stirring well.

Remove from the heat. Sir in the spring onions, shallots and pounded dry-fried rice. Turn into a bowl, garnish with coriander leaves and serve.

FRIED RICE WITH BASIL AND PRAWNS/SHRIMP (O)
KHAO PAD KRAPOW GUNG

This is Thai fast food, a typical quick lunch eaten by all business people and workers, cooked at road-side stalls or in restaurants. It is completely adaptable – you can substitute pork, chicken or any other meat for the prawns and vary the vegetables and spices at will.

2 tbsp vegetable oil
2 garlic cloves, finely chopped
2 small fresh red chilies, finely chopped
4 oz/120 g peeled raw prawns/shrimp
1 tbsp fish sauce
¼ tsp sugar
1 tbsp light soy sauce
20 fresh holy basil leaves
8 oz/240 g/1¼ cups boiled fragrant rice
1 small onion, slivered
½ red or green sweet pepper, slivered

In a wok or frying pan, over a high heat, heat the oil until a light haze appears. Add the garlic and fry until golden brown. Add the chilies and the prawns and stir quickly to mix. Add the fish sauce, sugar and soy sauce. Stir-fry until the prawns are cooked through. Add the basil leaves and stir. Add the cooked rice and stir thoroughly. Add the onion and the sweet pepper and stir quickly to mix. Turn on to a serving dish.

SPICY SWEETCORN CAKES WITH RICE VINEGAR PICKLE (HV)
TOD MAN KHAO POHD

3 large fresh sweetcorn-on-the-cob/ears of corn

1 tbsp red curry paste (page 89)

3 tbsp glutinous (sticky) rice flour

½ tsp salt

2 tbsp light soy sauce

1 tsp sugar

vegetable oil for deep frying

Run a knife along the lines of corn kernals to pull them away from the cob – you can use frozen sweetcorn though this will have been boiled and will give the 'cakes' a less authentic texture.

Place all the ingredients, except the oil, in a large bowl and knead together until thoroughly mixed into a thick paste. Form lumps of the paste into balls approx 1 inch/2.5 cm in diameter and then flatten them into patties.

Heat the oil to 200°C/400°F and deep fry the patties until golden brown. Drain on paper towels and serve hot with the following fresh pickle.

RICE VINEGAR PICKLE (D)
NAM JIM TUA

4 tbsp rice vinegar

2 tbsp sugar

½ tsp salt

3 inch/7.5 cm piece of English cucumber, sliced into rounds and then quartered

2 oz/60 g carrots, cut into rounds and then quartered

3 small shallots, finely sliced into ovals

3 small fresh red or green chilies, finely chopped

1 tbsp ground roasted peanuts

In a saucepan, heat the vinegar and dissolve in it the sugar and salt. Remove from the heat and allow to cool. Add the remaining ingredients and stir well. Pour into a bowl and serve with the sweetcorn cakes.

MANGO WITH STICKY RICE (K)
KHAO NIEW MAMUANG

8 fl oz/240 ml/1 cup coconut milk (page 178)

2 tbsp sugar

½ tsp salt

10 oz/300 g/1½ cups sticky rice, cooked and still warm

3 large ripe mangoes

2 tbsp coconut cream (page 178)

In a bowl, mix the coconut milk, sugar and salt, stirring until the sugar dissolves. Mix in the still warm cooked rice and set aside for 30 minutes.

Peel the mangoes and slice the two 'cheeks' of each fruit as close to the central stone/pit as possible. Slice each of these two pieces into quarters lengthways.

Mound the rice in the centre of a serving dish and arrange the slices of mango around it. Pour the coconut cream over the rice and serve.

NOODLES
GUEYTEOW

Noodles are a Chinese invention but have become the basic fast-food of most of Asia. In Thailand, we eat quite small bowls of noodles any time we feel peckish, getting them from the countless noodle-sellers that are one of the most noticeable features of Thai life. There are noodle stalls by the sides of busy streets, floating noodle boats on rivers, and even noodle trolleys built over bicycles which ply their trade up and down the narrow *sois*, or streets, of our cities, so that housewives and children can get some too. In Thailand, no one is far from a noodle-seller.

Noodles are made from either rice flour or soya bean flour and there are six main varieties:

1 *Sen yai*
Sometimes called 'rice river noodle' or 'rice sticks', this is a broad, flat, white rice flour noodle. Usually bought fresh, it is rather sticky and the strands need to be pulled apart before cooking. *Sen yai* can also be bought dried.
2 *Sen mee*
A small wiry looking rice flour noodle, this is usually sold dried and is sometimes called 'rice vermicelli'.
3 *Sen lek*
A medium flat rice flour noodle, usually sold dried. The city of Chantaburi is famous for *sen lek* noodles, which are sometimes called *Jantaboon* noodles after the nickname for the town.
4 *Ba mee*
An egg and rice flour noodle, medium yellow in colour, these come in a variety of shapes each with its own name. It is very unlikely that you will see anything other than the commonest form, which is thin and spaghetti-like, curled up in 'nests' which need to be shaken loose before cooking.
5 *Wun sen*
A very thin, very wiry, translucent soya bean flour noodle, also called 'vermicelli' or 'cellophane' noodle. Only available dried.

6 *Kanom jin*
The one uniquely Thai noodle, made from rice flour mixed with water, is squeezed through a special sieve to make thick strands like spaghetti. *Kanom jin* are only made in large quantities for special occasions, usually a communal task for a temple festival. Fortunately, there is a very similar Japanese noodle called *longxu* which is mass-produced and sold dried in packets in specialist shops.

Dried Noodles
All dried noodles, with the exception of *ba mee* noodles, need to be soaked in cold water for about 20 minutes before cooking (*wun sen* noodles require slightly less time). The dry weight will usually double after soaking, thus 4 oz/120 g dry noodles will produce 8 oz/240 g soaked noodles. After soaking they should be drained before cooking, which is usually a simple matter of dunking them in boiling water for 2 to 3 seconds or stir-frying them.

The Four Flavours *Kruang Prung*
While each noodle dish has its own distinctive taste, the final flavour is left to the diner, who can adjust it by sprinkling on quite small amounts of the Four Flavours. These are always put out in little bowls wherever noodles are served. The flavours are:
1 Chilies in Fish Sauce *Nam Pla Prik*: 4 small fresh red or green chilies, finely chopped, in 4 tbsp fish sauce.
2 Chilies in Rice Vinegar *Prik Nam Som*: 4 small fresh red or green chilies, finely chopped, in 4 tbsp rice vinegar.
3 Sugar *Nam Tan*
4 Chili Powder *Prik Pon*
▶

Noodles (*Gueyteow*) Top tray: *Sen yai*; *sen mee*. Bottom tray: Clockwise from top left: *Wun sen*; *ba mee*; *kanom jin*; *sen lek*. The Four Flavours: (*Kruang Prung*): Top to bottom: Chili powder (*Prik Pon*); chilies in fish sauce (*Nam Pla Prik*); chilies in rice vinegar (*Prik Nam Som*); sugar (*Nam Tan*).

RECIPES
WITH NOODLES

SPICY BEEF NOODLES WITH DRIED CHILIES (O)
GUEYTEOW PAD PRIK HAENG

From 1–3 feet (up to 1 metre) long, the aptly named long bean resembles an overgrown string bean, although it is of a different genus (see photograph on cover). However, because the taste is similar, the easier-to-find string bean can be used as a substitute, though the long bean has a crunchier texture and cooks faster. Choose darker rather than lighter coloured beans, preferably with smaller bean seeds inside the pods.

2 tbsp vegetable oil
2 garlic cloves, finely chopped
1–2 small dried chilies, finely sliced into rings
4 oz/120 g tender beef, thinly sliced
1 tbsp fish sauce
1 tbsp dark soy sauce
½ tsp sugar
2 oz/60 g/⅔ cup fresh beansprouts
2 oz/60 g long bean, chopped into 1 inch/2.5 cm lengths
3 oz/90 g *sen yai* noodles, soaked, rinsed and separated
fresh coriander leaves/cilantro, coarsely chopped, to garnish

In a wok or frying pan, heat the oil and fry the garlic until golden brown. Add the chilies and stir-fry for 2 seconds. Add the beef and stir well. Stirring quickly between each addition, add the fish sauce, soy sauce, sugar, beansprouts and long bean. Stir-fry until the beans are tender. Add the noodles and stir-fry until cooked through. Turn on to a serving dish and garnish with coriander leaves.

EGG NOODLES WITH SEAFOOD (O)
BA MEE NAH TALAY

1 nest *ba mee* noodles, fresh or dried
2 tbsp vegetable oil
2 garlic cloves, finely chopped
2 oz/60 g peeled raw prawns/shrimp
2 oz/60 g crab meat
2 oz/60 g cleaned baby squid, cut into rings
2 oz/60 g/¼ cup bamboo shoots, fresh or canned, sliced
8–10 straw mushrooms, fresh or canned, halved
1 tbsp light soy sauce
1 tbsp dark soy sauce
2 tbsp fish sauce
pinch of sugar
4 tbsp vegetable stock
ground white pepper
1 tbsp flour mixed with 2 tbsp water
1 spring onion/scallion, coarsely chopped

If using fresh noodles, shake the strands loose and set aside. Bring a saucepan of water to the boil. Using a coarse-meshed strainer or a sieve, dip either the fresh or the dried noodles into the boiling water. If fresh leave only for a few seconds; if dry, leave until the nest separates into strands in the water, at which point the noodles will be soft. Drain and set aside.

In a wok or frying pan, heat half the oil and fry half the garlic until golden brown. Add the noodles and stir-fry briefly until slightly darker and no longer wet. Turn on to a serving dish and keep hot.

Quickly heat the remaining oil in the pan and fry the remaining garlic until golden brown. Add the seafood and stir until cooked through. Add the bamboo shoots and straw mushrooms and stir. Add the light soy, dark soy, fish sauce, sugar, stock and a sprinkling of pepper, stirring briefly after each new addition. Add enough flour and water to thicken the mixture slightly; cook for 1–2 minutes. Add the spring onions, stir and turn on to the noodles. Serve.

THAI FRIED NOODLES (O)
PAD THAI

This is the best known of all Thai noodle dishes. The cause of its popularity has to be the range of ingredients and thus the wide variety of flavours and textures the dish contains. Once the ingredients are prepared it is very easy to make and the cooking time should not exceed 2–3 minutes. Because it is very copious, *Pad Thai* is usually served on its own, but I sometimes like to make up a special dinner party menu of interesting small dishes, in effect 'starters', brought out one after the other when ready, and then to offer a final dish of *Pad Thai* as a filler at the end of the meal.

2 tbsp vegetable oil
2 garlic cloves, finely chopped
1 size 2 egg/US extra large
6 oz/180 g *sen lek* noodles, soaked and drained
2 tbsp lemon juice
1½ tbsp fish sauce
½ tsp sugar
2 tbsp chopped roasted peanuts
2 tbsp dried shrimp, ground or pounded
½ tsp chili powder
1 tbsp chopped preserved radish/*chi po* (page 94)
1 oz/30 g/⅓ cup fresh beansprouts
2 spring onions/scallions, chopped into 1 inch/ 2.5 cm pieces
sprig of fresh coriander/cilantro, coarsely chopped
lemon wedges, to garnish

In a wok or frying pan, heat the oil and fry the garlic until golden brown. Break in the egg and stir quickly, cooking for a couple of seconds

only, then add the noodles and stir well, scraping down the sides of the pan to ensure that the egg and garlic are well mixed in. One by one, stirring between each addition, add the lemon juice, fish sauce, sugar, half the peanuts, half the dried shrimp, the chili powder, the preserved radish, 1 tablespoon of the beansprouts, and the spring onions. Test the noodles for tenderness and when they are *al dente* turn on to a serving dish. Arrange the remaining peanuts, dried shrimp and beansprouts around the noodle mixture. You can also put a little pile of chili powder and another of sugar on the side to be mixed in as each diner wishes. Garnish with coriander and lemon wedges and serve.

▶▶
Middle shelf: Egg Noodles with Seafood (*Ba Mee Nah Talay*); fresh pickle (*Adjahd*); Curried Rice and Chicken (*Khao Mok Gai*).
Bottom shelf: Mango with Sticky Rice (*Khao Niew Mamuang*).

33

SPICY PORK AND FISH BALL VERMICELLI NOODLE SOUP (O)
WUN SEN DU DEE

Du Dee is the name of a restaurant in Chantaburi which looks out over the park at the centre of the town. It is famous for its noodles – or rather its very *hot* noodles. On the menu they are marked 1 to 6 to show the degree of chili heat, and some of the higher ones also have names to encourage diners to feel proud of having braved the upper reaches – thus there are 'Rambo Noodles' and 'James Bond Noodles'. All of this is in sharp contrast to the name of the restaurant which can be roughly translated as 'Just fallen in love'. The chili level of the recipe here is pretty low by Thai standards, so if you want to get up to Rambo level you'll have to add a lot more – but take care!

4 oz/120 g piece of pork fillet/tenderloin
1 tbsp vegetable oil
1 garlic clove, finely chopped
½ pint/300 ml/1¼ cups chicken stock
1 tsp preserved vegetable/*tang chi* (see page 94)
3 oz/90 g *wun sen* noodles, soaked and drained
4 fish balls (fish and flour dumplings, bought ready-made in Chinese shops)
1 oz/30 g/⅓ cup fresh beansprouts
2 tbsp fish sauce
1 tsp sugar
½ tsp chili powder
1 tsp ground roasted peanuts
1 spring onion/scallion, chopped

Cook the piece of pork in simmering water for about 5 minutes. Drain and slice thinly. Set aside.

In a small pan, heat the oil and fry the garlic until golden brown. Remove from the heat and set aside.

In a saucepan, bring the stock and preserved radish to the boil. When at simmering point add the pork slices and all the other ingredients except the garlic. When the soup returns to the boil it is ready to serve: ladle into soup bowls and sprinkle a little of this garlic oil on to each portion.

CHICKEN FRIED NOODLES WITH CURRY PASTE (O)
SEN MEE PAD NAM PRIK GAENG

I have given a recipe for red curry paste on page 89, but you can buy it ready-made in Asian stores.

2 tbsp vegetable oil
2 garlic cloves, finely chopped
1 tbsp red curry paste (page 89)
6 oz/180 g boneless chicken, roughly chopped
3 oz/90 g *sen mee* noodles, soaked and drained
2 oz/ 60 g celery, roughly sliced
2 oz/60 g/⅔ cup fresh beansprouts
2 tbsp fish sauce
1 tbsp light soy sauce
1 tsp sugar

In a wok or frying pan, heat the oil and fry the garlic until golden brown. Add the curry paste and stir well. Add the chicken and stir-fry until cooked through. Add the remaining ingredients in turn, stirring well between each addition. Continue to stir-fry until the noodles are cooked *al dente*. Turn on to a serving dish and serve.

NAM PRIK CURRY NOODLES (OV)

KANOM JIN NAM PRIK

This recipe requires morning glory, or water spinach (see photograph on page 22), a vegetable slightly easier to find in North America than Europe. It has long jointed stems which remain firm when cooked, in contrast to the arrow-shaped leaves, which go limp. The flavour is slightly reminiscent of spinach. You should use it soon after purchase as the leaves quickly turn yellow and go bad. Watercress is a possible substitute.

8 oz/240 g white *longxu* noodles
4 oz/120 g long beans, finely chopped
4 oz/120 g fresh morning glory (water spinach), roughly chopped
4 oz/120 g/1¼ cups fresh beansprouts
2 large dried red chilies, coarsely chopped
The nam prik sauce:
4 tbsp vegetable oil
10 shallots, finely sliced into rings
5 garlic cloves, finely chopped
4 oz/120 g/½ cup dried split moong beans, soaked in water for 6 hours
2 coriander roots
1 tbsp red curry paste (page 89)
12 fl oz/360 ml/1½ cups coconut milk (page 178)
2 tbsp light soy sauce
1 tbsp sugar
1 tbsp tamarind water (page 142)
1 tbsp lemon juice
½ tsp chili powder
1 kaffir lime, cut in half
8 fl oz/240 ml/1 cup water

Boil the cluster of noodles until *al dente*. Drain and dip for a moment into cold water to stop the cooking. Drain again and place on to a serving dish. Set aside.

Bring a pan of fresh water to the boil and blanch the long beans, morning glory and beansprouts in turn, keeping them firm yet tender. Drain and place in heaps around the noodles. These will have cooled by the time the dish is served but that is not important.

For the sauce, heat half the oil and fry half the shallots and half the garlic until they are golden brown and crispy. Drain and set aside, retaining the oil for the side dish of fried dried chilies.

Drain the moong beans. Place in a mortar and pound to form a paste. Remove and set aside.

In the mortar, pound together the coriander roots with the remaining uncooked shallots and garlic until a paste forms. Set aside.

In a frying pan or wok, heat the remaining unused oil. Stir in the red curry paste and cook briefly. Add half the coconut milk, stirring well, then add the coriander root paste and stir again. Add the moong bean paste and stir well. Add the soy sauce, sugar, tamarind juice, lemon juice and chili powder, stirring constantly. Put the two halves of the kaffir lime into the mixture and continue to cook gently on a moderate heat for 10 minutes. Thin the remaining coconut milk with the water, then stir into the sauce and bring to the boil. Simmer for 1 minute. Quickly stir in the crisply fried shallot and garlic and immediately turn into a serving dish.

Reheat the oil used to fry the shallots and garlic. Quickly stir-fry the chilies. Turn into a small bowl. Serve as a side dish with the noodles and vegetables and *Nam Prik* sauce.

SAUCES

Four basic sauces are needed for Thai cooking. All are easily obtainable in the West, and if well sealed after use and used reasonably frequently, should keep with no difficulty.

Fish Sauce *Nam Pla*

This is the main flavouring for Thai cooking, for which there is no substitute. It is the salt of South East Asia, as indeed it was of Ancient Rome where a similar liquid called garum or liquamen was used before being replaced by salt. Although it can also be made with shrimps, fish sauce is most commonly the thin brown liquid extracted from salted, fermented fish. The best is home-made and has a light whisky colour and a refreshing salty taste rather than being dark with a heavy, bitter tang and a powerful fishy aroma.

When buying commercially produced fish sauce I try to find a lighter rather than a darker liquid. Colour is also the best way to judge whether a bottle has been open for too long as the sauce darkens with age. It should be discarded if it has changed colour significantly. Other than that, there is little to choose between the different producers and their country of origin – Thailand, Vietnam and China all produce good fish sauce. While some people prefer not to buy it in plastic containers, I doubt whether that makes any difference – go by the colour if anything.

▶

Sauces: Top to bottom: Bean sauce (*Tow Jiew*); fish sauce (*Nam Pla*); soy sauce (*Siew*); oyster sauce (*Nam Man Hoy*).

▼
Sun-drying squid in Rayong.

Soy Sauce *Siew* and **Bean Sauce** *Tow Jiew*
These are Chinese sauces made from soya
beans. Soy sauce is made from salted cooked
soya beans, fermented with flour, after which
the liquid is extracted. There are several
varieties and, while all are 'meaty' in flavour,
they vary in colour and intensity from light
brown to dark brown bordering on black.
Commercially, only two varieties are on offer:
light soy sauce, which is thin with a clear
delicate flavour, mild enough to be used as a
condiment at table, and *dark soy sauce* which is
thicker with a stronger sweeter flavour, having
been fermented with other ingredients such as
mushrooms and ginger that darken the final
liquid. However, the difference between light
and dark is slight, with dark being used more
to colour the food than anything. If you rarely
cook oriental food you will probably need
only a bottle of the more common light soy
sauce.

Bean sauces consist of slightly mashed
fermented soya beans – black or yellow. They
help thicken a dish as well as adding flavour.
Black bean sauce is thick and deeply coloured
and is used to give a richer flavour than even
dark soy sauce can achieve. *Yellow bean sauce* is
more salty and pungent but again, this is a
quite subtle refinement. If you only cook Thai
food occasionally you may need no more than
a jar of black bean sauce. You can, however,
get very small cans of both sauces, sufficient
for one Thai cooking session, and preservation
offers no problems as both bean sauces will
keep almost indefinitely if refrigerated.

Oyster Sauce *Nam Man Hoy*
This thick brown liquid is also of Chinese
origin and is made from oysters which have
been cooked in soy sauce and then mixed with
seasonings and brine. The result does not,
however, taste of fish, as might be expected.
It is sold in bottles and somewhat resembles
brown ketchup. If used rarely it should be
stored in the refrigerator.

RECIPES
WITH SAUCES

RAW PRAWNS/SHRIMP WITH SPICY FISH SAUCE (H)
GUNG CHAI NAM PLA

8 raw king prawns/jumbo shrimp, peeled and de-veined

4 tbsp fish sauce

2 tbsp lemon juice

1 tbsp sugar

5 small fresh red or green chilies, chopped

4 garlic cloves, sliced

Arrange the prawns on a bed of crushed ice.

In a small serving bowl, mix the fish sauce, lemon juice, sugar and chilies until the sugar has dissolved. Place the sliced garlic on a separate side plate. Serve the prawns with the sauce and the side plate of garlic – the diners should help themselves to the prawns, dipping them in the sauce and eating them with nibbles of raw garlic.

STEAMED SQUID WITH SOY SAUCE AND GINGER (T)
PLAMUK NUENG SIEW

2 tbsp vegetable oil

2 garlic cloves, finely chopped

8 oz/240 g baby squid, cleaned and chopped into rings

3 tbsp light soy sauce

1 inch/2.5 cm piece of fresh ginger, peeled and finely chopped

3 small fresh red or green chilies, finely chopped

1 tsp sugar

2 spring onions/scallions, chopped

Heat the oil in a small pan and fry the garlic until it is golden brown. Remove from the heat and set aside.

In a heatproof bowl, mix all the remaining ingredients, except the spring onions, stirring until the sugar has dissolved. Bring water to the boil in the bottom part of a steamer. Place the bowl in the top part of the steamer, cover and steam for 15 minutes.

Remove the bowl and turn the ingredients on to a serving dish. Pour over the reserved garlic oil, sprinkle with the chopped spring onions and serve.

42

DRIED BEEF WITH FISH SAUCE
(F)
NUA KEM

4 tbsp fish sauce

1 tsp sugar

7 tbsp vegetable oil

1 lb/480 g beef skirt or flank of steak, sliced diagonally across the grain into 8–10 pieces

Serve hot or cold as a snack with drinks or as an accompaniment to a hot curry.

In a medium-sized bowl mix the fish sauce, sugar and 1 tablespoon of oil. Add the pieces of beef and turn them in the mixture to coat all over. Leave to marinate for at least 1 hour.

Remove the meat and drain on a rack. In Thailand, after marinating, the meat would be sun dried. This can be simulated by leaving it overnight, or, if you cannot wait, by quick drying it in a warm oven or under a low grill/broiler, until all signs of liquid have gone, though without cooking it.

Heat the remaining oil in a wok or frying pan until a light haze appears, then stir-fry the dried meat on both sides until it is dark brown – about 5 minutes.

◀
Downtown Bangkok by night. The city has changed completely over the past twenty years and is now a thrusting metropolis poised between the old and the new.

▶
Boats come to Bangkok's central market, while across the Chao Phaya River the monumental Wat Arun, the temple of the Dawn, stands as a memorial to an older, more stately way of life.

ROAST CHICKEN WINGS WITH BLACK BEAN SAUCE (F)
PEEK GAI OP TOW JIEW

2 lb/960 g chicken wings

1 tbsp black bean sauce

1 tbsp light soy sauce

1 tsp sugar

3 garlic cloves, finely chopped

4 small fresh red or green chilies, finely chopped

½ tsp ground white pepper

In a roasting dish, mix all the ingredients, ensuring that the chicken wings are well coated. Leave to marinate for at least 1 hour.

Preheat the oven to 350°F/180°C/gas mark 4. Roast the chicken wings for about 30 minutes.

CHILI FISH SAUCE (D)
NAM PLA PRIK

2 tbsp fish sauce

2 tsp lemon juice

4 small fresh red or green chilies, finely chopped

Mix together in a small bowl and serve.

FRIED CURRIED AUBERGINE/EGGPLANT WITH YELLOW BEAN SAUCE (FV)
PAD PET MAKUA TOW JIEW

2 tbsp vegetable oil

2 garlic cloves, finely chopped

1 tbsp red curry paste (page 89)

1 large dark purple aubergine/eggplant, halved lengthways and thinly sliced across

6 tbsp vegetable stock

1 large red sweet pepper, seeded and chopped

2 tsp yellow bean sauce, drained to remove excess liquid

1 tbsp light soy sauce

1 tbsp sugar

20 fresh holy basil leaves

In a wok or frying pan, heat the oil and fry the garlic until golden brown. Stir in the curry paste, then add the aubergine slices and stir-fry for 5 minutes. Stir in the stock and add all the remaining ingredients except the basil. Simmer for 5 minutes. Stir in the basil leaves and serve at once.

PRAWN/SHRIMP WITH ASPARAGUS AND OYSTER SAUCE (F)
GUNG PAD NAM MAN HOY

2 tbsp vegetable oil

2 garlic cloves, finely chopped

6 oz/180 g raw prawns/shrimp, peeled and de-veined

6 oz/180 g young thin asparagus, chopped into 2 inch/5 cm lengths

2 tbsp oyster sauce

1 tbsp fish sauce

½ tsp sugar

½ tsp ground white pepper

In a wok or frying pan, heat the oil and fry the garlic until golden brown. Stirring constantly, add each of the remaining ingredients in turn, stirring well between each addition. When the prawns are pink and opaque turn on to a serving dish and serve.

YELLOW BEAN SAUCE WITH CRUDITÉS (D)
TOW JIEW LON

For the crudités, any crisp fresh vegetables will do – cucumber, Chinese/Napa cabbage, long beans, etc.

crisp vegetables of your choice
The dip:
4 oz/120 g/⅔ cup yellow bean sauce, drained to remove excess liquid
8 fl oz/240ml/1 cup coconut milk (page 178)
2 small shallots, finely chopped
4 oz/120 g minced/ground pork
1 tbsp tamarind water (page 142) or 2 tbsp lemon juice
2 tsp sugar
1 tbsp fish sauce
2 large fresh red chilies, sliced lengthways into fine matchsticks

Chop the crudités into small, convenient portions, arrange on a serving platter and set aside.

In a mortar, briefly pound the drained yellow beans until broken up; set aside.

In a saucepan, heat the coconut milk, then add the mashed yellow beans and stir well. Add all the other dip ingredients, with the exception of the chilies. Bring to the boil and simmer briefly. Remove from the heat, stir in the chili matchsticks, turn into a bowl and serve with the crudités.

FRIED RICE WITH BEEF AND DARK SOY SAUCE (O)
KHAO PAD SIEW

1 tbsp vegetable oil
2 garlic cloves, finely chopped
4 oz/120 g minced/ground lean beef
1 egg
8 oz/240 g/1¼ cups boiled fragrant rice
2 oz/60 g/⅓ cup broccoli, coarsely chopped
1 tbsp dark soy sauce
1 tbsp light soy sauce
pinch of sugar
1 tbsp fish sauce
ground white pepper

Heat the oil in a wok or frying pan over a high heat. Add the garlic and fry until golden brown. Add the beef and stir-fry briefly. Break the egg into the mixture and stir well. Add the rice and stir, then add the broccoli and stir into the mixture. Stirring constantly, add the dark soy, light soy, sugar and fish sauce. Give the mixture a final stir, turn on to a serving dish, shake ground white pepper over to taste, and serve.

If you want to spice up this dish you can serve a little bowl of Chili Fish Sauce (opposite) as an accompaniment.

BEANCURD
TAO HOU

Beancurd or tofu is the nearest oriental cooking gets to a dairy product, although it is of course entirely vegetable based. It is cheap and easy to use, but as its flavour is bland, it must be combined with other, tastier ingredients. Beancurd is produced from the water extract of yellow soya beans which are soaked and then pulverized in water; the solids are filtered out and the remaining liquid is briefly cooked to remove unwanted chemical elements. The addition of powdered calcium carbonate causes the liquid to curdle. The curd is poured into cloth-lined trays about 12 inches/ 30 cm square or into plastic boxes. The curd solidifies into a shiny white block, ready to be cut into smaller squares for cooking. In Thailand, both hard and soft beancurd is available, but in the West only soft beancurd in liquid can be found easily and this is the variety used in the following recipes. Basic soft beancurd is easily obtainable from Chinese stores, health food shops and many supermarkets. It is sold in its own liquid which should be discarded before cooking. Beancurd is very delicate, and it is preferable to buy and use it at once, although it is possible to keep fresh beancurd for a maximum of three days provided you pour away and replace the water each day.

Other forms of beancurd are:

Ready Fried Beancurd *Tao Hou Tod*
White beancurd which has been deep-fried a golden brown on the outside. Available from Chinese shops.

Beancurd Sheets *Fong Tao Hou*
Bought dried in packets, these look like wrinkled brown paper. They are very fragile but after soaking for 5-6 minutes they should pull apart fairly easily. Any torn sections can be patched with other pieces. Available from Chinese shops.

Red Beancurd *Tao Hou Yee*
This is a pickled or fermented beancurd, sold in jars. It has a very strong pungent flavour and is used in sauces.

◄
A floating market near Bangkok – Thailand's rivers were once its principal highways and are still the best way to transport food from farm to table.

►
Beancurd (*Tao Hou*)
Top to bottom: Fresh white beancurd (*tao hou kow*); tinned red beancurd (*tao hou yee*); beancurd sheets (*fong tao hou*); ready fried beancurd (*tao hou tod*).

BEANCURD AND FISH BALL SOUP (S)

GAENG JUED TAO HOU LU SIN PLA

Fishballs are a form of *quenelles* or dumpling made with flour and fish. They are about ½ inch/1.25 cm in diameter and are sold ready-made in oriental stores.

The amount here will serve up to four.

16 fl oz/500 ml/2 cups chicken stock
2 tbsp fish sauce
1 tbsp light soy sauce
1 tsp preserved vegetable/*tang chi* (see page 94)
½ tsp ground white pepper
4 oz/120 g beancurd, cut into 16 x ½ inch/1.25 cm cubes
8 fish balls
2 spring onions/scallions, green part only, cut into 1 inch/2.5 cm slivers

In a medium saucepan, heat together the chicken stock, fish sauce, soy sauce, preserved vegetable and white pepper. When simmering, add the cubes of beancurd and the fish balls. Cook for 30 seconds, then add the pieces of spring onion. Simmer for a few seconds. Ladle into small bowls and serve.

BEEF AND VERMICELLI SOUP WITH RED BEANCURD SAUCE (O)

SUKI NUA

4 oz/120 g tender boneless beef, finely sliced
1 tbsp fish sauce
1 tbsp light soy sauce
½ tsp sugar
1 egg
sprinkling of ground white pepper
The sauce:
1 tbsp red beancurd
1 tbsp lemon juice
1 tsp fish sauce
1 tsp light soy sauce
1 tsp sugar
2 pickled garlic cloves/*kratiam dong* (page 98), finely chopped
2 small fresh red or green chilies, finely chopped
For the soup:
1 pint/600 ml/2½ cups beef stock
2 oz/60 g/heaped ½ cup Chinese leaf/Napa cabbage, coarsely chopped
2 oz/60 g/½ cup celery (with some leaf), chopped
2 spring onions/scallions, chopped diagonally into 1 inch/2.5 cm pieces
1 tbsp fish sauce
1 tbsp light soy sauce
2 oz/60 g *wun sen* noodles, soaked and drained

Put the beef, fish sauce, soy sauce, sugar, egg and pepper in a bowl. Mix well and leave to marinate while preparing the sauce.

Place all the sauce ingredients in a bowl and whisk with a fork until smooth. Set aside.

For the soup, bring the stock to the boil in a saucepan. Add the marinated beef and any remaining marinade, return to the boil and simmer until the beef is just cooked through. Add the vegetables, fish sauce and soy sauce and stir. Still stirring, add the noodles and cook for 2–3 seconds (the noodles become soft very quickly). Turn into a serving bowl.

Ladle a little soup into each diner's bowl. Serve the sauce separately so that each diner may stir in as much as required.

FRIED STUFFED BEANCURD (H)
TAO HOU YAT SY

2 oz/60 g minced/ground pork
2 oz/60 g minced/ground raw prawns/shrimp
2 garlic cloves, finely chopped
1 tbsp fish sauce
½ tsp ground white pepper
8 oz/240 g ready-fried beancurd
vegetable oil for deep frying
5 tbsp rice vinegar
4 tbsp sugar
1 tsp salt
½ tsp chili powder
2 tsp ground roasted peanuts
fresh coriander leaves/cilantro, to garnish

In a bowl, mix the pork, prawns, garlic, fish sauce and pepper to make a stuffing. Set aside.

Take the cubes of fried beancurd and open each one by making a slice along one side. The interior should be hollow, but you may need to gently push back the soft curd to make a slightly larger space. Stuff the cubes with the pork mixture.

Heat a pan of oil for deep frying to 400°F/200°C. Deep fry the stuffed beancurd cubes, turning once. You will be able to see the stuffing and gauge when it is cooked through – this should not take more than 2 minutes. Drain on paper towels and place on a warm serving dish.

In a saucepan, heat the vinegar, sugar and salt until the mixture thickens. Remove from the heat and add the chili powder and ground peanuts, stirring well until thoroughly mixed. Turn into a serving bowl, garnish with coriander leaves and serve with the stuffed beancurd.

HOT AND SOUR CRISPY BEANCURD SALAD (YV)
YAM TAO HOU GROB

3 oz/90 g beancurd sheets
vegetable oil for deep frying
1 garlic clove, finely chopped
4 small fresh red or green chilies, chopped
2 tbsp lemon juice
2 tbsp light soy sauce
1 tsp sugar
1 oz/ 30 g carrot, cut into 1 inch/2.5 cm matchsticks
1 onion, finely sliced
1 tbsp crushed roasted peanuts
fresh coriander leaves/cilantro, to garnish

Soak the beancurd sheets in water to cover for 5–6 minutes. Drain and separate the sheets. Dry on paper towels.

Heat a pan of oil for deep frying to 400°F/200°C. Deep fry the beancurd sheets until golden and crispy. Drain on paper towels. Roughly break them into a salad bowl. Add all the other ingredients and toss well. Sprinkle with coriander and serve.

Top and bottom left:
Raw prawns/shrimp and (below) ingredients for Raw Prawns with Spicy Fish Sauce (*Gung Chai Nam Pla*).
Top right: Fried Stuffed Beancurd (*Tao Hou Yat Sy*).
Bottom right: Roast Chicken Wings with Black Bean Sauce (*Peek Gai Op Tow Jeow*).

BEANCURD WITH VEGETABLES AND BLACK BEAN SAUCE (FV)
LAHD NAH TAO HOU

6 tbsp vegetable oil

8 oz/240g beancurd, cut into ½ inch/1.25 cm cubes

2 garlic cloves, finely chopped

4 oz/120 g/½ cup broccoli, roughly chopped

4 oz/120 g mangetout/snow peas

1 tbsp light soy sauce

1 tsp black bean sauce

½ tsp sugar

pinch of ground white pepper

6 tbsp vegetable stock

½ tsp cornflour/cornstarch, mixed with a little water

Heat 4 tablespoons of the oil in a wok or frying pan and fry the cubes of beancurd until golden brown. Drain and set aside.

Heat the remaining oil in the pan and fry the garlic until golden brown. Stirring constantly, add the vegetables, soy sauce, black bean sauce, sugar and pepper. Stir-fry, adding the vegetable stock little by little, until the broccoli stems are tender. Finally, blend in the cornflour mixture to thicken slightly. Serve hot.

STEAMED BEANCURD SHEET STUFFED WITH CHICKEN (T)
FONG TAO HOU HAW GAI

Dried black fungus mushrooms (cloud ears or *champignons noirs*) are the commonest Asian mushroom, usually bought dried in 2 oz/60 g packets. They should be soaked in water at room temperature until soft (20–30 minutes). The smaller the mushrooms the better, and do remember to test any new brand you buy to be sure it is free of sandy grit.

4 beancurd sheets (approx 6 x 12 inches/ 15 x 30 cm)

6 oz/180 g/1 cup boneless chicken, finely diced

1 oz/30 g dried black fungus mushroom, soaked then roughly sliced

2 oz/60g/⅓ cup bamboo shoots, roughly sliced

2 garlic cloves, finely chopped

2 tbsp soy sauce

1 tsp sugar

½ tsp ground white pepper

Soak the beancurd sheets in water to cover for 5-6 minutes. Drain and separate the sheets carefully. Set aside.

In a bowl, mix all the other ingredients to make a stuffing. Divide the stuffing into 4 equal portions. Place a portion of stuffing at the centre of a beancurd sheet. Fold one corner over the stuffing, then fold over the other corners in turn to make an envelope.

Arrange the envelopes on a heatproof plate with the folds underneath to hold them down. Bring water to the boil in the bottom part of a steamer. Place the plate in the top part of the steamer, cover and steam for 15 minutes.

BEANCURD WITH CRAB AND CHILIES (F)
——— BU PAD PRIK TAO HOU ———

6 tbsp vegetable oil

8 oz/240 g beancurd, cut into ½ inch/1.25 cm cubes

2 garlic cloves, finely chopped

4 oz/120 g white crab meat

4 oz/120 g baby sweetcorn, roughly chopped

2 spring onions/scallions, roughly chopped

2 large fresh chilies, sliced lengthways

2 tbsp light soy sauce

1 tbsp fish sauce

1 tsp sugar

½ tsp ground white pepper

1 tsp cornflour/cornstarch, mixed with a little water

Heat 4 tablespoons of oil in a wok or frying pan and fry the beancurd briefly until it just begins to change colour. Remove with a slotted spoon and set aside.

Heat the remaining oil in the pan and fry the garlic until golden brown. Stirring constantly, add the crab meat, then the fried beancurd cubes, sweetcorn, spring onions, chilies, soy sauce, fish sauce, sugar and pepper. Stir thoroughly. Stir in the cornflour mixture to thicken the sauce slightly, then serve.

SPICY BEANCURD WITH MINCED PORK (F)
——— CHU CHEE TAU HOU MOO SAP ———

vegetable oil for deep frying + 2 tbsp oil

8 oz/240 g beancurd, cut into ½ inch/1.25 cm cubes

1 tbsp red curry paste (page 89)

4 oz/120 g minced/ground pork

2 tbsp fish sauce

1 tsp sugar

4 tbsp chicken stock

2 tbsp ground roasted peanuts

2 kaffir lime leaves, rolled up like a cigarette and sliced across into fine slivers

Heat a pan of oil for deep frying to 400°F/200°C. Deep fry the beancurd cubes until golden brown. Drain on paper towels and arrange on a serving dish. Set aside.

Heat the 2 tablespoons of oil in a wok or frying pan and briefly fry the curry paste, stirring constantly. Add the minced pork and stir-fry until it is no longer pink. Add the fish sauce, sugar and stock, mixing well. Add the peanuts and kaffir lime leaf slivers. Reduce the heat and simmer until the sugar thickens the sauce.

Pour the sauce over the deep-fried beancurd and serve.

SHRIMPS

GUNG

Both dried shrimps and shrimp paste are used as salty flavourings.

Dried Shrimps *Gung Haeng*

These are not preserved shrimps waiting to be reconstituted in water and used as a seafood ingredient in a dish. Instead they should be considered more as a dry flavouring that is especially good with blander ingredients such as cabbage and beancurd. Ideally, dried shrimps should be tiny, a natural shrimp pink and not too salty. This flavouring is made by boiling and peeling shrimps and then spreading them out in the sun to dry. The end result is sold loose, in jars or in plastic bags. Dried shrimps can be kept for a long time though they may go slightly moist, in which case they must be either sun dried again or dry heated briefly in an oven.

Look out for a special variant from the southern city of Songkla. These shrimps are not peeled but are dried in their shells. They are very good deep fried, after which the shells are crispy and edible; these are then served as an appetizer.

Shrimp Paste *Kapee*

Because it is full of protein and is a good source of vitamin B, shrimp paste is a staple for many of Asia's poor who survive on a diet of boiled rice, flavoured with this pungent preserve. The paste is made by pounding shrimps with salt and leaving them to decompose. It is sold both dried and 'fresh', a slight misnomer when what is really meant is 'not dried'.

The 'fresh' *kapee* is shrimp pink and can be bought in jars in the West, though it is difficult to find. It can be stored in the refrigerator. The sun-dried variety is dark purple from the black eyes of the *kheu* shrimp, but be wary if it is too dark as this may mean that dye has been added. Dried *kapee* is stronger than fresh, but once again it should not be painfully salty. Rayong produces the best dried *kapee*. It can be kept without refrigerating.

Both fresh and dried shrimp paste have a disturbingly powerful aroma and you should remove what you want from the jar as quickly as possible lest you create a bad smell in your kitchen. Fortunately this odour disappears when the *kapee* is cooked.

You can use either fresh or dried shrimp paste in a recipe. Unless otherwise stated, my recipes all call for dried *kapee*. If substituting fresh, use double the quantity of dried. If none can be found you could use Western anchovy paste – about half the amount of the dried shrimp paste required.

◄

Aubergines/eggplant Common large purple aubergine; long light green aubergine; pea aubergine; small round green aubergine; small yellow aubergine.

▶

Shrimp paste (*Kapee*); dried shrimps (*Gung Haeng*).

HOT AND SOUR DRIED SHRIMP AND MANGO SALAD (Y)
YAM GUNG HAENG

1 unripened small green mango, approx 4 oz/ 120 g

2 tbsp vegetable oil

4 oz/120 g dried shrimps

4 small fresh red or green chilies, finely chopped

3 shallots, finely chopped

2 garlic cloves, finely chopped

2 tbsp lemon juice

2 tbsp fish sauce

1 tsp sugar

Do not peel the mango. Cut it into thin slices, working around the stone/pit. Finely sliver the slices into thin matchsticks and set aside.

Heat the oil in a small pan and fry the shrimps until they begin to brown. Drain on paper towels and put in a salad bowl. Add the mango and all the other ingredients, and toss well until thoroughly dressed. Serve.

STICKY RICE WITH DRIED SHRIMPS (H)
KHAO NIEW NUNG BAI BUA

The Thai name for this dish is more accurately translated as 'sticky rice with dried shrimps *in lotus leaves*', because in Thailand the mixture is steamed in a lotus leaf cup. This imparts a special flavour during cooking. As it is almost impossible to get lotus leaves in the West I have radically adapted the recipe, but feel happy that it has sufficient echoes of the original to merit being here.

8 oz/240 g/1¼ cups sticky rice

2 tbsp vegetable oil

2 garlic cloves, finely chopped

½ tsp salt

4 oz/120 g dried shrimps

Soak the sticky rice in water to cover for 3 hours; drain. Heat the oil in a wok or frying pan and fry the garlic until golden brown. Add the sticky rice, salt and dried shrimps, and stir well while frying briefly. As soon as the ingredients are thoroughly mixed, transfer to a heatproof bowl.

Bring water to the boil in the bottom part of a steamer. Place the bowl in the top part of the steamer. Cover and steam for 30 minutes. Serve hot.

LADBURI NOODLES WITH HARD-BOILED EGG AND DRIED SHRIMPS (O)
GUEYTEOW LADBURI

1 tbsp vegetable oil

1 garlic clove, finely chopped

3 oz/90 g *sen lek* noodles, soaked and drained

1 oz/30 g/⅓ cup fresh beansprouts

1 oz/30 g dried shrimps

1 tbsp fish sauce

1 tsp sugar

1 tbsp ground roasted peanuts

1 hard-boiled egg, cut into wedges

1 spring onion/scallion, finely sliced into rings

In a small pan, heat the oil and fry the garlic until golden brown. Remove from the heat and set aside.

Heat a saucepan of boiling water. Place the noodles in a sieve or strainer and dip them into the water for 5 seconds. Drain and place them in a large bowl. Repeat the procedure with the beansprouts to blanch them. Drain and put them in the bowl. Repeat the procedure with the dried shrimps; drain and add to the bowl.

Mix the noodles, beansprouts and shrimps together. Pour over the garlic and oil mixture and mix well. Add the fish sauce, sugar and peanuts and mix well. Turn on to a dish, garnish with wedges of hard-boiled egg and sprinkle with spring onion. Serve with the Four Flavours (page 30).

GRILLED AUBERGINE/EGGPLANT WITH DRIED SHRIMPS (Y)
YAM MAKUA POW

1 medium-size dark purple aubergine/eggplant, weighing about 8 oz/240g

1 tbsp dried shrimps, lightly pounded to a rough-grained powder

10 small shallots, finely sliced

2 medium-size spring onions/scallions, finely chopped

3 tbsp lemon juice

2 tbsp fish sauce

1 tsp sugar

5 small fresh red or green chilies, finely chopped

fresh coriander leaves/cilantro, to garnish

Wrap the whole aubergine in foil and place under a hot grill/broiler for 15 minutes, turning from time to time. Remove the foil. Cut away the stalk and peel away the skin with the edge of a knife. Slice the aubergine lengthways into quarters then crossways twice to make 12 pieces. Place in a bowl and pour in all the remaining ingredients. Stir just enough to coat the aubergine, but taking care not to mash the flesh too much. Turn on to a plate and garnish with coriander leaves.

Unusually, this *yam* is always served with rice, so it could be considered a main course rather than a salad.

Left: Smoking fish the old way.

Right: Recipes with shrimps (*Gung*)
Top left and centre: Deep Fried Fish with Spicy Shrimp Paste (*Pla Tod Nam Prik Kapee*): Bottom right: Sticky Rice with Dried Shrimps (*Khao Niew Nung Bai Bua*).

SMOKED FISH WITH FRIED SHRIMP PASTE (F)
KAPEE TOD

In Thailand I would buy ready-smoked catfish for this recipe, but in the West, smoked mackerel is a perfectly good substitute and is, of course, easily obtainable.

1 tbsp finely chopped tender lemon grass
1 tbsp finely chopped krachai
1 tbsp finely chopped coriander root
2 small shallots, finely chopped
2 tsp dried shrimp paste
8 oz/240 g smoked fish fillet (such as mackerel), roughly broken into small fragments
2 tbsp/30 ml vegetable oil + more for deep frying
1 tbsp fish sauce
1 tbsp light soy sauce
1 tsp sugar
½ tsp ground white pepper
1 egg

Place the lemon grass and krachai in a large mortar and pound with a pestle until well broken up. Add the coriander root, shallots, shrimp paste and smoked fish and continue pounding until a paste is formed.

In a wok or frying pan, heat the oil and add the paste. While stirring, add the fish sauce, soy sauce, sugar and pepper, mixing well. Remove from the heat and leave to cool.

When cold, divide the cooked paste into small balls ½ inch/1.25 cm in diameter and flatten each into a 1 inch/2.5 cm diameter patty. Break the egg into a bowl and whisk to mix. Heat a pan of oil for deep frying to 400°F/200°C.

Dip each patty into the egg and then deep fry briefly, turning once, until the egg coating is golden. Drain on paper towels and serve.

SHRIMP PASTE CURRY (C)
GAENG LIANG

Although I have called this a curry, it is really an in-between dish, as much a hot stew as anything, but used to perk up a meal rather as a curry would be. It is 'pepper' hot rather than 'chili' hot.

1 tbsp white peppercorns
10 small shallots
1 tbsp dried shrimp paste
4 tbsp dried shrimps
1 litre/1¾ pints/4 cups chicken stock
3 tbsp fish sauce
4 oz/120 g courgettes/zucchini, halved lengthways then cut into 1 inch/2.5 cm pieces
4 oz/120 g baby sweetcorn, halved with a diagonal cut
10 fresh holy basil leaves

Place the peppercorns, shallots and shrimp paste in a mortar and pound together to form a paste; remove and set aside. Clean the mortar. Pound half the dried shrimps to a fine powder and set aside. In a large saucepan, heat the stock, stir in the paste and bring to the boil. Add the shrimp powder and the remaining whole dried shrimps and stir well. Add all the remaining ingredients and stir well. Simmer until the courgettes are just cooked *al dente*. Turn into a bowl and serve.

DEEP FRIED FISH WITH SPICY SHRIMP PASTE (D)
PLA TOD NAM PRIK KAPEE

This is a version of *Nam Prik*, the spicy dip that is one of the classic dishes of Thailand. Everyone has their version and people take great pride in serving their own special flavour.

You can eat a wide variety of things with *Nam Prik* – cooked and raw vegetables as well as deep-fried fish – so having mastered this basic recipe you should try to vary it by adding a little more chilli or fish sauce or lemon juice to see what pleases you most, then start to vary the things you serve with it, depending on what is in season.

I have suggested the pea aubergine, the very small green eggplant common in Asia, though still quite rare in Europe and North America. The pea aubergine is only slightly larger that a garden pea. There is another variety of small round green aubergine which is about 1 inch/ 2.5 cm in diameter. Because they are hard and crunchy, these vegetables add a special texture to a dish and thus cannot be replaced by the common dark purple aubergine which is very soft when cooked. The only possible substitute is the slightly harder, long, thin, pink-skinned aubergine/eggplant, though this too is quite rare in the West.

seasonal raw vegetables such as thin green beans cut into 2 inch/5 cm lengths, slivers of carrot, celery and cucumber, etc.

vegetable oil for deep frying

1 pomfret or 3 sardines, cleaned

The spicy dip:

2 garlic cloves, chopped

5 small fresh red or green chilies

1 tbsp dried shrimp paste

3 tbsp fish sauce

3 tbsp lemon juice

1 tbsp sugar

2 tbsp crushed pea aubergines/eggplant (if available)

Preheat the grill/broiler.

In a mortar, pound the garlic with the chilies and set aside. Grill/broil the shrimp paste on a piece of foil for 2 minutes, then put it into the mortar and pound with the chilies and garlic. Add the remaining ingredients and pound into a paste. Turn into a small bowl, place in the centre of a large platter and surround with the vegetables.

Heat a pan of oil for deep frying. Deep fry the whole fish, turning once, until it is crisp and golden brown. Drain on paper towels and add to the platter. Serve immediately.

FRIED PORK WITH SHRIMP PASTE (F)
MOO PAD KAPEE

2 tbsp vegetable oil

2 garlic cloves, finely chopped

8 oz/240 g boneless pork, roughly sliced

2 tsp dried shrimp paste

4 small fresh red or green chilies, finely chopped

5 round green aubergines/eggplants (see photograph on page 54), quartered

2 tbsp fish sauce

1 tbsp lemon juice

1 tbsp sugar

In a wok or frying pan, heat the oil and fry the garlic until golden brown. Add the pork and stir-fry until just cooked through. Stirring constantly, add all the remaining ingredients in turn and, after stirring in the sugar, serve.

2

THE SEARCH FOR SHANGRI-LA

◆

THE NORTH AND THE GOLDEN TRIANGLE

I f you are visiting the northern capital Chiang Mai and you want a delicious lunch, all you have to do is hail a *samloh*, a bicycle rickshaw, and ask the driver to take you to Pen's restaurant. If he complains that there are too many Pens, just say *'Pen Tam Som'* and he'll know exactly where you mean. *Tam Som* is Mrs Pen's personal version of the spicy northern dish, *Som Tam*, which is usually made with grated raw papaya pounded with garlic, nuts, beans and chilies. Instead of the papaya Mrs Pen uses pomelo, the large fruit very similar to a grapefruit. Without giving that clue to the *samloh* driver, the restaurant would be hard to find, as it is simply part of Mrs Pen's house in the family compound on Chaa Bahn Road behind the Gong Muang police station. This is not untypical of some of the best Thai restaurants, which are often small family affairs, run by one or two people who specialize in a particular home-made dish that makes them famous locally. Mrs Pen only cooks at lunchtime; in the evening her son Tom takes over, serving drinks with the highly flavoured northern dishes that visitors from Bangkok love so much – *Gaeng Nua*, a northern curried fish, and *Nam Prik Num*, a highly spiced dip.

For many years, Chiang Mai remained a safe retreat from the chaos of Bangkok, but now it too is undergoing mammoth development and rapid change. There is still, however, the cooler cleaner mountain air and the lush valleys nearby, with their elephant trails and winding paths that trekkers take up into the golden triangle. This is the wild, mountainous region that lies across the borders of Thailand, Burma and Laos, inhabited by hill tribes who still follow their traditional ways, largely untouched by the modern world which encloses them. An eleven-hour winding road journey west from Chiang Mai will bring you to the nearest you can get to Shangri-La: the little town of Mae Hong Son, nestling in a deep valley near the Burmese border and ringed with majestic wooded mountains. The town has a number of Burmese-style temples with multi-tiered roofs that loom out of the thick morning mists which often blanket the valley, adding to its mysterious air of dreamy isolation.

There is Burmese influence too, in the food of the north, especially in the rich and chewy curried noodles, *Kow Soi*. These noodles are so sumptuous they are almost as addictive as the opium that is still grown in the surrounding mountains, despite the government's efforts to suppress it. The lack of success is partly due to agriculture, for the hill tribes' traditional slash and burn method of farming so denuded the land that eventually they could only scratch a living out of cultivating poppies. The best attempts at preventing drug production have been those that try to reintroduce better

◄◄
A misty mountain morning in Mae Hong Son as a woman earns merit by offering food to the passing monks.

farming methods, which will help feed the tribespeople and give them produce they can sell to the towns.

One such project is in Doi Tung near Chiang Rai, a city about 200 kilometres north of Chiang Mai. It was set up by the mother of Thailand's present king who had flown over the area and seen the devastation left by traditional hill tribe farming. Now, about 45,000 acres of steep slopes have been terraced and linked with hairpin roads so that coffee can be grown and transported to the southern markets. Reforestation is underway and there are plant nurseries where the basic ingredients for flavouring Thai food – garlic, shallots, chilies – are again being cultivated.

Many southern Thais are attracted to the wilder, freer life of the mountains, away from the concrete valleys of the big cities. The last time I was up in Chiang Rai, I visited the extraordinary home of one of Thailand's most famous artists, Towan Datchanee, whose strange surrealist paintings of creatures – half-man, half-beast – have a haunting quality derived from the misty heights at which he has chosen to live. This is also reflected in his home, a compound of traditional wooden stilt houses, painted the deep black and rich red of the hill tribes' costumes and furnished with alarmingly spiky chairs made out of buffalo horns. More horns decorate the gardens outside, perched on high totem poles, and there are buffalo skulls set into the earth. The artist himself wears a necklace of bone and teeth. It is strange to reflect that while the royal family and the government are trying to persuade the hill tribe peoples to enter the modern economy, supposedly sophisticated Thais are eagerly going back to a primitive past.

It is the distant past that draws many visitors to the north, in search of the ancient ruined cities, monuments to the kingdoms that rose and fell, through wars and invasions. The most spectacular, Sukhothai, lies halfway between Bangkok and Chiang Mai, and was once the centre of the first truly Thai kingdom. Its spectacular ruins and giant Buddhas sitting serenely in the open air bear mute witness to the first uniquely Thai art, which set its stamp on all that was to follow. To wander around the ruins by moonlight is an awesome experience. Even better is to see it lit by thousands of candles during the Loi Kratong festival at the close of the rainy season, when tiny candle-lit rafts are launched on to the rivers and canals that criss-cross the site of the ancient city.

As the power of Sukhothai waned, so that of independent Chiang Mai rose. Indeed it was not until this century that the area around Chiang Mai was completely absorbed into the Thai nation.

66 There is still a sense of 'otherness' that makes it the preferred destination for southern Thais wanting to enjoy both the envigorating climate and the special food for which the north is justly famous. Most foreign visitors have to try a *Kahn Toke* dinner, a set meal laid out on a special raised tray that holds bowls containing *Nam Prik Ong*, a spicy dip eaten with crispy pork and raw vegetables; *Ook Gai*, chicken and lemon grass curry; *Laab*, spicy ground beef; and sticky rice. The diners take scoops of rice with their fingers and use these to carry portions of the other food to their mouths in traditional style.

If you go to Lamphun, 26 kilometres south of Chiang Mai, once the centre of the ancient Haripunjaya kingdom, take the Salapee Road and look out for the Sawai Riang resort, a charming group of old stilt houses built around an artificial lake, at the centre of which is a floating restaurant where people go to relax, drink and nibble highly spiced local delicacies. Pickles and preserves are a speciality of the region and many of these are used to create richly flavoured dishes such as *Ped Toon Manow Dong* (duck with lime pickle) which is just the thing to waken up a jaded palate.

Sawai Riang is a tranquil haven in a changing world, where natural beauty seems ever harder to find. There is, however, a sign of hope for the future, which you will see on your drive out of Chiang Mai: the tall trees that line the Salopee Road. At one time these trees had bright saffron-coloured clothes tied around the trunks. The reason for this is fascinating: apparently, the government decided that the rapid development of the region necessitated the widening of the road and thus the felling of these old trees, which had been planted in the last century by order of King Chulalongkorn the Great, one of whose wives came from the region. To shade her journey along this route, to and from Bangkok, the king had commanded that the planting take place. The villagers were angered that a gentle act of royal courtesy should be cast aside in this way. Their solution was ingenious – they simply declared that the trees had become monks and wrapped them in the same saffron cloths that real monks wear. When any workman turned up to chop down a tree the villagers would demand to know why he intended to 'kill' a monk. This soon drove the workmen away. For once it was local people fighting to save their natural environment, rather than having conservation imposed upon them from above. I am happy to say the authorities finally gave in and decided to build another road on the other side of the trees, leaving the king's gift to his wife intact.

▶
The Golden Triangle. A hill-tribe woman harvests the opium poppy.

GARLIC AND SHALLOTS

KRATIAM, HOM DAENG

Garlic is an essential part of the great majority of Thai dishes. It is used whole, chopped, crushed, raw, fried and pickled. Thai garlic cloves are small with a thin papery skin, which is why we often do no more than crush them with a heavy blow of the side of a cleaver before tossing them, skins included, into the pan. With non-Thai garlic you will have to peel off the skin. If a recipe specifies 2 garlic cloves you should adjust this if you have the sort of large bulbous garlic usually associated with French or Italian cooking.

The first use of garlic in Thai cooking is to flavour the cooking oil before frying meat or vegetables. We never use oils, such as olive oil, that carry their own flavour, and we only rarely use sesame oil. For the most part we prefer bland vegetable oils in which a little garlic is fried to impart a flavour before the rest of the ingredients are added.

Some dishes call for garlic to be fried in a little oil until golden brown and then reserved to be sprinkled over the finished dish almost like a final pungent condiment.

In the main, garlic is a hidden flavour, but sometimes it moves to centre stage, cut into ovals and deep fried to add a rich taste and crisp texture. Where a really strong flavour is required we use pickled garlic, which I have included in the section on pickles (page 98).

Buy garlic that is firm to the touch and seems heavy for its size; a slight pinkish tinge is a good sign. Garlic keeps well in a cool, dry, well-ventilated place, but should not be stored in the refrigerator where it may become mildewed or start to sprout. Whole, peeled garlic cloves can be kept for several months in a sealed jar.

The shallot is a sweeter and milder member of the onion family. Thai shallots are so sweet we sometimes use them in desserts. Shallots are best when small, with copper-red skins that need to be peeled like ordinary onions. Some varieties come in tight clusters like large garlic cloves, and need to be pulled apart. Avoid the very large varieties that sometimes appear, as these can be as strongly flavoured as the average onion, which rather misses the point. Small shallots are sold loose or tied in bundles. They should be firm and without any sprouts or blemishes or signs of rot. Like garlic they keep well in a cool, dry, ventilated place, but may sprout in the refrigerator.

RECIPES
WITH GARLIC AND SHALLOTS

GRILLED MUSHROOMS WITH GARLIC AND CHILI SAUCE (HV)
HET HOM YANG

Chinese dried mushrooms (*shiitake*) are almost the same shape as the common Western large flat mushroom, though they are slightly smaller and tougher in texture. They should be soaked in water at room temperature for about 20 minutes, the water squeezed out and the tough stalk removed.

4 oz/120 g dried Chinese mushrooms/*shiitake*
4 garlic cloves, roughly chopped
3 coriander roots, roughly chopped
1 tsp ground black pepper
1 tbsp sugar
1 tbsp light soy sauce
The sauce:
1 tbsp sugar
6 tbsp rice vinegar
1 tsp salt
1 garlic clove, crushed
3 small fresh red or green chilies, finely chopped

Soak the mushrooms in water to cover for 1 hour; drain and pat dry. Pull off and discard the stalks. Carefully cut the cap of each mushroom into one long spiral, from the rim to the centre, as if peeling an apple in a single strip. Set aside.

In a mortar, pound the garlic and coriander roots to make a thick paste. Stir in the pepper, sugar and soy sauce. Pour the mixture over the mushroom strips and leave to marinate for 30 minutes.

Meanwhile, make the sauce. Place the sugar, vinegar and salt in a small pan and heat gently. Cool slightly, then stir in the garlic and chilies and set aside.

Preheat the grill/broiler. Remove the mushroom strips from the marinade and thread on to bamboo skewers (it is advisable to first soak the skewers in cold water for 20–30 minutes so that they do not burn). Place the skewers under the grill and cook for 1–2 minutes on each side or until sizzling and dark brown. Serve at once, with the dipping sauce.

FRIED CHICKEN WITH GARLIC AND SESAME SEEDS (F)
GAI GNA KRATIAM

2 tbsp sesame oil
4 garlic cloves, thinly sliced
1 large dried red chili, thinly sliced
8 oz/240 g boneless chicken breast, roughly chopped
1 tbsp fish sauce
1 tbsp light soy sauce
3 spring onions/scallions cut into 2 inch/5 cm lengths
1 tbsp dry-fried sesame seeds, use the same method as for dry-frying rice (page 24)

In a wok or frying pan, heat the oil and fry the garlic until golden brown. Add the chili and briefly stir-fry, then add the chicken and stir well. Add the fish sauce and light soy sauce, and stir. Add the spring onion and stir well. As soon as the chicken is cooked through, stir in the sesame seeds, turn on to a plate and serve.

Garlic (*Kratiam*) and Shallots (*Hom Daeng*)
In pan: Garlic, fried golden brown. Below: Raw shallots.
On chopping board: Whole garlic; garlic cloves; finely chopped garlic and whole crushed garlic clove.

72

FRIED FISH WITH CRISPY GARLIC (F)
PLA TOD KRATIAM KROP

1 lb/480 g white fish fillets (cod or haddock)

3 tbsp cornflour/cornstarch

½ tsp salt

vegetable oil for deep frying

fresh coriander leaves/cilantro to garnish

The sauce:

2 tbsp vegetable oil

5 garlic cloves, thinly sliced

1 tbsp finely chopped fresh ginger

1 tbsp light soy sauce

1 tbsp fish sauce

½ tsp sugar

1 tbsp white vinegar

3 tbsp chicken stock or water

Rinse the fish fillets, pat dry and coat lightly with the cornflour mixed with the salt. Heat a pan of oil for deep frying to 400°F/200°C. Deep fry the fish until golden on both sides. Drain on paper towels and set aside.

In a wok or frying pan, heat the oil and fry the garlic until dark golden and crispy. With a slotted spoon or sieve remove the garlic from the oil and set aside. Add the remaining sauce ingredients to the pan and stir well.

Pour the sauce over the fish, sprinkle the crispy garlic on top, garnish with coriander and serve.

CHIANG MAI SAUSAGE (H)
NAM

1 lb/480 g boneless piece of pork with skin, a slice of leg or loin would do

6 garlic cloves, finely chopped

1 tsp salt

2 oz/60 g/6 tbsp cooked fragrant rice

5–6 small whole fresh chilies

To serve:

small lettuce leaves

roasted peanuts

shallots, quartered

garlic cloves, quartered

small fresh red or green chilies, chopped

fresh coriander leaves/cilantro, coarsely chopped

lemon wedges for squeezing

Carefully cut the skin, not the fat, from the meat. Place the skin in a saucepan, cover with water and boil for 15 minutes. Drain and dice very small.

Remove and discard most of the fat from the meat then mince/grind it. Thoroughly mix the pork with the finely diced skin, the garlic, salt, cooked rice and chilies. Press down with the hand to ensure the mixture is as compressed as possible, then shape into a sausage and roll tightly in clingfilm/plastic wrap. Roll again in foil (we would traditionally use a banana leaf). The sausage should be as firm as possible. Tie with string or rubber bands and leave in the refrigerator for 3 days to cure.

After 3 days, unwrap the sausage and cut into ¼ inch/5 mm slices. Serve with the suggested accompaniments. To eat, place a piece of sausage on a lettuce leaf, add any or all of the accompaniments, roll up the leaf and eat.

BEEF WITH GARLIC AND GREEN PEPPERCORNS (F)
NUA TOD KRATIAM PRIK TAI SOD

2 tbsp vegetable oil
4 garlic cloves, thinly sliced
8 oz/240 g lean tender steak
½ tsp ground white pepper
1 tbsp fish sauce
1 tbsp light soy sauce
2 stems of fresh whole green peppercorns

In a wok or frying pan, heat the oil and fry the garlic until brown and crispy. Remove the garlic with a slotted spoon or sieve and set aside. Fry the whole piece of steak to taste (preferably rare). Remove the steak and slice it thinly. Place in a bowl and add all the other ingredients, pulling the peppercorns off their stems. Add the crispy garlic, mix thoroughly, turn on to a dish and serve.

BARBECUED SPARE RIBS (H)
GRAT DOO MOO YANG

1 lb/480 g pork spare ribs
4 garlic cloves, finely chopped
1 tbsp finely chopped coriander root
1 tbsp oyster sauce
1 tbsp light soy sauce
1 tbsp fish sauce
1 tsp sugar
1 tsp ground white pepper

In a large bowl, mix all the ingredients thoroughly together, making sure the spare ribs are well coated. Leave to marinate for at least 1 hour.

Cook the spare ribs over charcoal, about 15 minutes each side. The tiny, thin spare ribs from young piglets will need less. Any remaining marinade can be poured over the ribs while they are cooking.

PRAWNS/SHRIMP IN HOT AND SOUR SALAD (H)
GUNG MAE PING

lettuce, cucumber, radish and fresh coriander leaves/cilantro, to garnish
8 oz/240 g large raw prawns/shrimp, peeled and de-veined
4 tbsp chicken stock
2 tbsp fish sauce
4 tbsp lemon juice
1 tsp chili powder
1 tsp sugar
4 shallots, finely sliced
1 tbsp dry-fried rice (page 24), roughly pounded

Prepare a serving plate with the lettuce, cucumber, radish and coriander leaves.

Preheat the grill/broiler. When very hot, grill/broil the prawns until just cooked through. Set aside.

In a small pan, combine the stock, fish sauce, lemon juice, chili powder and sugar. Bring to the boil over a high heat, stirring constantly. When boiling, add the prawns and stir, then add the shallots and stir again. Add the dry-fried rice, stir, and cook for a few seconds. Turn into the centre of the prepared serving plate and serve.

74 STEAMED EGG AND SHALLOTS (T)
KAI TOON HOM DANG

Fish balls are a form of *quenelle* – a dumpling made with fish and flour rolled into a ball. These are already cooked when you buy them and are simply reheated when you cook the dish. Fish balls and meat balls are available from all Chinese stores.

3 size 2 eggs/US extra large
6 oz/ 180 g fish balls
3 shallots, finely chopped
2 tbsp fish sauce
1 tsp ground white pepper
4 tbsp water
1 tsp finely chopped fresh coriander/cilantro

Heat the water in the bottom of a steamer to boiling.

Break the eggs into a heatproof bowl. Add the fishballs, shallots, fish sauce, pepper and water and lightly beat together. Add the coriander and stir in.

Place the bowl in the upper part of the steamer, cover and steam for 12–15 minutes or until the egg is set and the tines of a fork inserted into the mixture come out with no liquid on them.

The bowl should be placed on the table with a serving spoon so that each diner can take a little as required. An impressive alternative is to steam a small individual bowl or ramekin for each diner.

▶
Steamed Egg and Shallots (*Kai Toon Hom Dang*).

HOT AND SOUR CHICKEN AND SHALLOT SOUP (S)
TOM KONG

16fl oz/500 ml/2 cups chicken stock

2 whole chicken wings, on the bone, roughly chopped into 1 in/2.5 cm pieces

5 shallots, peeled

2 large dried red chilies

2 tbsp fish sauce

1 tbsp lemon juice

1 tsp sugar

20 fresh sweet basil leaves

Preheat the grill/broiler.

In a saucepan, heat the stock. Add the chicken pieces and bring back to the boil, then leave to simmer. Meanwhile, place the shallots and the chilies under the grill and grill/broil until the chilies begin to blacken, turning once. Transfer the grilled shallots and chilies to a board. With the handle or side of a large kitchen knife, crush them until they split open. Add the crushed shallots and chilies to the pan of stock and continue to simmer until the chicken pieces are cooked through.

Throw in the fish sauce, lemon juice, sugar and basil leaves. Stir quickly and serve at once.

BROCCOLI STEMS WITH CRISPY SHALLOTS (Y)
YAM KNAA

2 tbsp vegetable oil

5 shallots, thinly sliced lengthways

8 oz/240 g broccoli stems, roughly chopped (the florets can be used for another dish)

3 garlic cloves, finely chopped

1 tsp finely chopped small fresh red or green chilies

1 tbsp Grilled Chili Oil/*Nam Prik Pow* (page 84)

2 tbsp coconut cream (page 178)

6 oz/180 g cooked boneless chicken, without skin, finely shredded

2 tbsp fish sauce

2 tbsp lemon juice

2 tbsp chicken stock or water

1 tbsp sugar

2 tbsp ground roasted peanuts

In a wok or frying pan, heat the oil and fry the shallots until golden brown and crispy. With a slotted spoon or sieve remove from the oil and set aside.

Bring a saucepan of water to the boil and blanch the broccoli stems for 5 seconds. Drain and set aside.

Reheat the oil in the wok or frying pan and fry the garlic until golden brown. Add the chilies and stir. Mix in the *Nam Prik Pow* and then the coconut cream. Add the chicken and stir, then add the broccoli stems and stir. Stirring constantly, add the fish sauce, lemon juice, chicken stock or water, sugar and ground roasted peanuts. Finally, stir in the crispy shallots and serve.

BEEF, POTATO AND SHALLOT SOUP (S)
TOM JIEW

16 fl oz/500 ml/2 cups chicken stock

6 oz/180 g tender boneless beef, cut into 1 inch/2.5 cm cubes

4 oz/120 g potato, cut into 1 inch/2.5 cm cubes

2 tbsp shallots, finely sliced lengthways

1 tbsp tamarind water (page 142)

2 tbsp fish sauce

1 tsp sugar

4 small fresh red or green chilies, slightly crushed with the side of a kitchen knife

20 fresh sweet basil leaves

In a large pan, heat the chicken stock to boiling. Add all the remaining ingredients and simmer until the potatoes are cooked *al dente*. Pour into a tureen and serve.

NORTHERN CURRY (C)
GAENG NUA

1 medium-sized mackerel or similar firm-fleshed oily fish, cleaned, head and tail removed

16 fl oz/500ml/2 cups chicken stock

5 shallots, peeled and slightly crushed with the side of a large kitchen knife

5 garlic cloves, peeled and slightly crushed as above

1 inch/2.5 cm piece of galangal, peeled and slightly crushed as above

1 stalk of lemon grass, chopped into 4 pieces and slightly crushed as above

2 inch/5 cm piece of krachai, peeled and cut into fine matchsticks

2 large dried red chilies, roughly chopped

2 tbsp pickled fish/*pla raa*

1 tbsp fish sauce

1 tsp sugar

Cut the mackerel across into 2 inch/5 cm chunks. Set aside.

In a large pan, heat the stock to boiling. Add the fish and all the other ingredients, stirring well. Bring back to the boil and simmer until the fish is cooked through but still firm. Pour into a tureen and serve.

CHILIES
PRIK

There are said to be more than 300 members of the *capsicum* family, which includes the large sweet peppers used as vegetables down to the small thin hot chilies that are used as spices. Of the latter, there are more varieties than I could possibly list, though Thai cooking calls mainly for the categories described here, plus the two by-products that follow.

Chilies were discovered in South America in the sixteenth century by the Spanish who took them home, from whence they spread to Portugal, whose sailors carried them out to India and South East Asia. They completely transformed the local cuisines wherever they appeared, for while the Indians and the Thais had always eaten 'hot' food, they had used mustard seed and black and white peppercorns,

which were as nothing when compared to the fiery little fruit, to which millions became addicted. It is sobering to reflect on the fact that the chili's burning flavour is a form of natural defence and that no animal except man dares eat it. All sorts of reasons are advanced as to why some peoples ingest such quantities of it – usually said to be a help in coping with a hot climate or as a way of dealing with bad meat in the tropics – but none of these stands up to examination. The simple fact is that hot food is addictive and that once you are used to highly spiced and chili-flavoured meals, all else seems bland and uninteresting.

Aware of the sensibilities of Western palates, I have moderated the chili levels in my recipes, but not so much as to make them any less realistically Thai. If you can stand them, add more chilies; if you can't, then you can always remove the seeds before cooking – this will leave some of the flavour and almost none of the heat.

Do be very careful when handling chilies. If you do not wear rubber gloves then be sure to wash hands and implements thoroughly afterwards and be careful never to rub your eyes or other sensitive places – don't dare go to the lavatory – before making sure that all trace of the little fruit has been scrubbed from your hands!

◄
A million chilies come to market!

►
Chilies (*Prik*)
Top left: *Prik khee noo*.
Centre: *Prik haeng*.
Right: *Prik khee noo suan*. Bottom compartment: Red and green *Prik chee faa* and yellow *Prik yuak*.
Below left: Chili sauce (*Sod prik*). Right: Chili powder (*Prik pon*).

80 The main varieties of chili used in Thailand are:

1 *Prik khee noo suan*
The name for these tiny red or green chilies (about ½ inch/1.25 cm long) translates as 'mouse dropping'. They are much appreciated for their intense heat. Because they do not keep well, you are unlikely to find them outside South East Asia, as exporters prefer to send the next largest size.

2 *Prik khee noo*
Slightly larger, at about 1 inch/2.5 cm long, these fresh red or green chilies are marginally less hot but still pretty fiendish.

3 *Prik chee faa*
These fresh red or green chilies are about 3–4 inches/7.5–10 cm long. They are slightly less hot than the small varieties.

4 *Prik yuak*
This is the largest of the hot chilies. It is a pale-yellow green and broad in shape, similar to our sweet or bell peppers though thinner. It is closest to a Hungarian white paprika, so if you cannot find the Thai variety you could substitute one of these or even an ordinary sweet pepper.

5 *Prik haeng*
Large dried red chilies, hotter than *prik chee faa*. These are sun-dried, deep maroon/red and about 3–4 inches/7.5–10 cm long.

Selecting chilies is not easy and Thai cooks tend to nibble whatever is on offer to test freshness and piquancy – a method not recommended to the uninitiated! With fresh chilies you should look out for firmness and an unblemished skin. Other than that you will just have to deal with a supplier you can trust as there are no set guidelines. Fresh chilies in a sealed jar will keep in the refrigerator for up to a week. Stored in an airtight container, out of direct sunlight, dried chilies will keep for several months.

The following chili products are used as condiments to heighten the flavour of a dish.

Chili powder *Prik pon*
A red powder made by grinding small dried red chilies (*prik khee noo haeng*). In Thailand it is sold in jars, packets or cardboard containers.

Chili sauce *Sod prik*
A thick dipping sauce made from a combination of sweet and hot chilies, pulped and mixed with vinegar, garlic and other spices.

RECIPES
WITH CHILIES

CHIANG MAI SPICY DIP (DV)
NAM PRIK NUM

2 large fresh green chilies
4 small fresh green chilies
4 large garlic cloves, peeled
4 small shallots, peeled
2 medium-size tomatoes
5 round green aubergines/eggplants (page 61)
2 tbsp lemon juice
2 tbsp light soy sauce
½ tsp salt
1 tsp sugar

Preheat the grill/broiler.

Wrap the first 6 ingredients in foil and place under the grill. Cook until they begin to soften, turning once or twice. Unwrap, place in a mortar and pound together to form a liquid paste. In turn, add the remaining ingredients to the paste, stirring well.

Turn into a small bowl. Serve surrounded by a selection of salads, crispy lettuce, cucumber, radish, celery or by raw or blanched vegetables.

STUFFED HOT PEPPERS (T)
PRIK SOD SY

If you cannot find the Thai variety of chili pepper, you can substitute 2 ordinary large sweet peppers.

3 large fresh yellow-green peppers/*prik yuak*
3 garlic cloves, finely chopped
1 tbsp finely chopped coriander root
8 oz/240 g minced/ground chicken
2 tbsp red curry paste (page 89)
1 egg
2 tbsp fish sauce
1 tbsp light soy sauce
½ tsp sugar
3 kaffir lime leaves, finely chopped

Cut the peppers in half lengthways and remove the seeds.

In a mortar, pound the garlic with the coriander root. Add the other ingredients and pound to make a paste. When thoroughly mixed, spoon loosely into the pepper cups. Do not pack down or they will dry out. Bring water to the boil in the bottom part of a steamer. Place the peppers in the top part of the steamer, cover and steam for 15 minutes. Serve hot.

In mortar: Chiang Mai Spicy Dip (*Nam Prik Num*).
Front left: Stuffed Hot Peppers (*Prik Sod Sy*).
In frying pan: Fried Beef with Chili (*Nua Pad Prik*).

FRIED BEEF WITH CHILI (F)
NUA PAD PRIK

2 tbsp vegetable oil

2 garlic cloves, finely chopped

2 large fresh red chilies, slivered lengthways

1 tsp black bean sauce

8 oz/240 g tender boneless beef, finely sliced

1 medium-size onion, halved and sliced

1 tbsp fish sauce

1 tbsp light soy sauce

1 tsp sugar

In a wok or frying pan, heat the oil and fry the garlic until golden brown. Add the remaining ingredients in turn, stirring between each addition. Stir-fry until the beef is just cooked through. Turn on to a plate and serve.

GRILLED CHILI OIL
NAM PRIK POW

I have kept the word 'Grilled' as part of the name for this dish as we still use it in Thailand even though we now fry the ingredients. This is not so much a separate dish as a relish. It can be eaten alone, on bread, as if it were a fiery jam! But it is more often added to other dishes such as soup, to buck up the flavour. Because it is used to make *tom yam* soup, it is sometimes known as *tom yam* sauce. *Nam prik pow* is used as an ingredient in the following dishes: Hot and Sour Pork Salad, Fried Prawns with Grilled Chilies and Waterchestnuts (both on page 85), Broccoli Stems with Crispy Shallots (page 76) and Hot and Sour Soup with Prawns/Shrimp (page 133).

4 tbsp vegetable oil

4 tbsp finely chopped garlic

4 tbsp finely chopped shallots

4 tbsp finely chopped large dried red chilies

2 tbsp dried shrimps

1 tsp salt

1 tbsp sugar

In a wok or frying pan, heat the oil and fry the garlic until golden brown. Remove the garlic with a fine sieve and set aside. Add the shallots to the oil and fry until brown and crispy; remove with the sieve and set aside. Add the chilies to the oil and fry until they begin to darken; remove with the sieve.

In a mortar, pound the dried shrimps, then add the chilies, garlic and shallots and pound until thoroughly blended. Add this to the oil and stir over a low heat. Add the salt and stir to mix. Add the sugar and mix to make a thick, slightly oily, red/black sauce, not a paste.

Hot and sour pork salad (Y)
PLA MOO

This dish can be treated as a *yam* salad, and could be served as a first course or as a snack with drinks.

8 oz/240 g boneless pork, roughly chopped
2 tbsp chicken stock
1 tbsp Grilled Chili Oil/*Nam Prik Pow* (opposite)
1 stalk of lemon grass, trimmed of all tough leaves, finely sliced into rings
4 small round green aubergines/eggplants (page 61), sliced into rounds
2 shallots, finely sliced
3 kaffir lime leaves, finely chopped
2 small fresh red or green chilies, finely chopped
1 tbsp fish sauce
2 tbsp lemon juice
1 tbsp sugar
The marinade:
2 garlic cloves, finely chopped
1 tbsp oyster sauce
1 tbsp fish sauce
1 tbsp light soy sauce

Put all the marinade ingredients in a large bowl and stir well. Add the pork and leave to marinate for at least 1 hour.

Preheat the grill/broiler. Arrange the marinated pork on a rack set over a pan to catch the juices and grill/broil until cooked, turning as necessary.

In a saucepan, heat the stock to boiling. Stir in the *Nam Prik Pow* and add the pork with any juices. Stir in the remaining ingredients, mixing well. Turn on to a serving dish.

Fried prawns/shrimp with grilled chili oil and waterchestnuts (F)
GUNG PAD PRIK POW

2 tbsp vegetable oil
2 garlic cloves, finely chopped
4 long dried red chilies/*Prik haeng*, roughly chopped
8 raw king prawns/jumbo shrimp, peeled and de-veined
1 tbsp Grilled Chili Oil/*Nam Prik Pow* (opposite)
4 oz/120 g/1 cup waterchestnuts, finely diced
1 tbsp light soy sauce
1 tbsp fish sauce
½ tsp sugar

In a wok or frying pan, heat the oil and fry the garlic until golden brown. Add the chilies and stir, then add the prawns and stir well. Add the remaining ingredients in turn, stirring constantly. When the sugar has been stirred in, turn on to a dish and serve.

SPICES
KRUEN TET

It is perhaps surprising to learn that the spices most commonly associated with exotic cooking – cloves, cumin, cardamom, etc. – are rarely used in Thai cuisine. Even our curries are made from fresh herbs and vegetables rather than being spiced with the dried aromatic seeds and roots that are used in Indian curries. Spices have edged into Thai cuisine via the south where there is a large Muslim population, many of Malaysian origin. From them we have taken Mussaman or Muslim curry, which is highly spiced in the Indian/Arabic manner. But apart from that one exception, the Thai use of spices is sparing, and they are only added to a dish to give a specific, rather 'foreign' flavour, much as a Western cook might add a dash of hot pepper sauce.

Cloves *Kaan Ploo*
These are imported from a variety of sources – Moluccas (Indonesia), Zanzibar (Tanzania), India and Sri Lanka. They can be bought whole or ground into a powder. While the whole ones keep well, ground cloves do go musty and you are better off pounding whole ones in a mortar as needed. Whole cloves impart a strong refreshing flavour to meat and poultry, especially duck, where the sharp almost antiseptic clove flavour counteracts the heavy, rich flavour of the meat.

Coriander Seeds *Luk Pak Chee*
These are round, like peppercorns, and when dried give off a sweet orange aroma that actually improves the longer the seeds are kept. You should buy them whole and grind when needed. Keep them in a sealed jar away from direct sunlight.

Cumin *Yeeraa*
Originally from Egypt, cumin seeds are central to North African cooking and also feature in Indian curries. They need to be heated to release their aromatically spicy flavour. While you can buy ground cumin, it will lose both its flavour and aroma within 2 months.

◄
Chiang Mai's central market is an assault on the eye and the nose but a treasure-house of flavours.

►
Spices (*Kruen tet*)
Top to bottom, left to right:
Star anise (*Dok Jan* or *Poy Kat*); cinnamon (*Ob Chuey*); nutmeg (*Luk Chand*); cloves (*Kaan Ploo*); cardamom – green and brown – (*Luk Kravan*); cumin (*Yeeraa*); curry powder (*Pung Gari*); five spices (*Haa Kruen Tet*); coriander seeds (*Luk Pak Chee*).

88

Cinnamon *Ob Chuey*

Cinnamon sticks are the rolled up, thin sheets of the inner bark of a laurel-like tree, native to Sri Lanka but now found in India and elsewhere. You can also buy ground cinnamon. While it will not stay fresh as long as the sticks, it is so difficult to grind cinnamon sticks that for once you are probably well advised to take this short-cut.

Star Anise *Dok Jan* or *Poy Kat*

The prettiest of all the spices, this is a dried star-shaped, red-brown fruit. It figures prominently in Cantonese cuisine. In Thailand we use it in pork dishes that have a Chinese influence. It is the principle ingredient of five-spice powder.

Nutmeg *Luk Chand*

Well known in the West, nutmeg was once so loved that people carried their own with them, to flavour food and drinks. The nut contains myristicin, which has an effect not unlike mescalin – take enough and you can have hallucinations! Nutmegs are either dark brown or white-limed. You can test for quality by pressing the nut hard – a little oil should appear on the surface. Keep whole nutmegs in an airtight container and grate a little when needed, as ground nutmeg does not keep.

Cardamom *Luk Kravan*

Cardamom is an expensive spice – historically it was used as an ingredient for perfumes and as an aphrodisiac. Because of the demand there are a number of cardamom-related plants that are often sold as the real thing. These have a strong camphor flavour. Jars of the spice may contain the substitutes mixed in with real ground cardamom, so it is better to buy whole ones and to grind your own. Real cardamom pods are green, brown or bleached white. You need to break them open to extract the black seeds, which are then pounded or ground. (Cardamom leaves are occasionally used as a flavouring, but they are hard to find even in Thailand; however, you can use bay leaves as a substitute.)

Five Spices *Haa Kruen Tet*

This is much used in Chinese, especially Cantonese, cuisine and is easily obtainable from Chinese shops. The mixture should contain peppercorns, fennel, cloves, cinnamon, and star anise. Some versions replace the peppercorns with ginger, making a much sweeter blend that is often used in desserts.

The mixture will almost certainly be sold in a sealed pack so you will have no way of testing its aroma, which should be both spicy and sweet at the same time.

Curry Powder *Pung Gari*

Thai cooks like short-cuts as much as any others and one way of adding instant 'dash' to a dish is to include a little 'curry powder' (see photograph on page 87).

This is seldom explained in Thai cookbooks, probably because the ready-prepared curry powder generally on sale in Thailand is the standard yellow variety. In Europe and North America, however, there are many others now available, so a guide is helpful. You are best advised to use a mild Madras curry powder, which is saffron-coloured and contains as its primary ingredients: coriander, turmeric, mustard, Bengal gram, cumin, chilies, fennel, pepper, garlic and salt.

RECIPES
WITH SPICES

BITTER MELON CURRY (C)
GAENG OM MA RAD

The quantities given here will make roughly 10 tablespoons of curry paste. We will need only 2 tablespoons for this recipe, so store the remainder in a sealed container in the refrigerator (not freezer). You could use this paste instead of the red or green curry paste in some of the other curry recipes in this book, to give a slightly different flavoured curry.

1 bitter melon, weighing about 10 oz/300 g
2 tbsp vegetable oil
16 fl oz/500 ml/2 cups coconut milk (page 178)
6 oz/180 g fresh oyster mushrooms
2 tbsp light soy sauce
1 tsp sugar
2 large fresh red chilies, cut diagonally into thin ovals
The red curry paste/Nam Prik Gaeng Daeng:
5 large dried red chilies, seeded and roughly chopped
1 tsp salt
1 tsp finely chopped galangal
1 tbsp finely chopped tender lemon grass
3 tbsp finely chopped garlic
3 tbsp finely chopped shallots
1 tbsp coriander seeds
1 tsp cumin seeds
1 tsp dried shrimp paste

For the curry paste, put the chilies in a mortar and pound them well. Add the remaining ingredients in turn, pounding constantly to form a thick paste.

Cut the bitter melon lengthways into 4 slices and then cut across into ¼ inch/5 mm pieces. Set aside.

In a wok or frying pan, heat the oil, stir in 2 tablespoons of curry paste and fry for a few seconds. Add the coconut milk and stir until the liquid begins to reduce and thicken. Add all the other ingredients in turn, stirring well between each addition. Turn into a bowl and serve.

ROAST DUCK WITH CLOVES (F)
PED YANG

1 duckling, weighing about 4 lb/1.85 kg
5 cardamom leaves (bay leaves may be substituted)
4 garlic cloves, roughly chopped
2 coriander roots, finely chopped
2 tbsp light soy sauce
1 tbsp dark soy sauce
1 tsp sugar
1 tsp ground white pepper
10 whole cloves

Preheat the oven to 425°F/220°C/gas mark 7.

Place the cardamom or bay leaves inside the duck. In a bowl, mix together all the other ingredients except the cloves. When well mixed, smear the resulting paste over the duck as evenly as possible. Stick the cloves into the duck as evenly spaced as you can manage. Place the duck on a rack in a roasting pan.

Roast for 20 minutes, then turn the heat down to 350°F/180°C/gas mark 4. Continue roasting for 2 hours, occasionally pouring away any excess fat. After removing from the oven, leave the duck to 'relax' for 5 minutes before carving.

▶▶
Hanging at rear: Roast Duck with Cloves (*Ped Yang*). In sacks: Star anise and cinnamon sticks. On scales: Cloves. At front in saucepan: Bitter Melon Curry (*Gaeng Om Ma Rad*). In 'golden' wok: Pork Belly with Five Spices (*Moo Pa Low*).

SUN-DRIED BEEF WITH CORIANDER SEED AND CUMIN (H)
NUA SAWAN

1 tbsp coriander seeds
1 tbsp cumin seeds
1 lb/480 g lean tender beef steak, thinly slivered
1 tbsp salt
1 tbsp palm sugar
vegetable oil for deep frying

Roughly pound the coriander and cumin seeds in a mortar with a pestle. Do not pound to a powder.

Place all the ingredients, except the oil, in a bowl and turn well to coat the beef (use your fingers!). Lay the well-coated slices of beef on a plate and leave in intense sunlight to dry. Alternatively, dry overnight on a rack placed over a pan in a low oven, until all the juices have gone but before actual cooking commences.

Heat a pan of oil for deep frying to 400°F/200°C. Deep fry the dried beef slices until dark. Drain on paper towels and serve.

BEEF STEWED WITH CINNAMON AND STAR ANISE (S)
GOW LAO NUA PEUI

This dish can be served with the Four Flavours (page 30), so that the diners can adjust the piquancy to their own taste.

1¾ pints/1 litre/4 cups beef stock
1 lb/480 g lean boneless beef, cut into ½ inch/1.25 cm cubes
3 garlic cloves, roughly chopped
3 coriander roots
2 cinnamon sticks
4 star anise
2 tbsp light soy sauce
2 tbsp fish sauce
1 tsp sugar
4 oz/120 g/½ cup fresh beansprouts
1 spring onion/scallion, finely chopped
fresh coriander leaves/cilantro, roughly chopped, to garnish

Put the stock into a large saucepan. Add the beef, garlic, coriander roots, cinnamon, star anise, soy sauce, fish sauce and sugar. Bring to the boil and simmer for 30 minutes. Skim off the scum occasionally.

In the meantime, put the beansprouts into a serving bowl.

Pour the hot soup over the beansprouts, garnish with chopped spring onion and coriander and serve.

MUSSAMAN CURRY (C)
GAENG MUSSAMAN

The word Mussaman is the Thai version of Muslim. It was Muslim settlers in the south of the country who introduced elements of Malaysian cuisine into Thailand, of which this curry is the best known example. Its popularity may also be due to the fact that it is one of the rare dishes in Thai cooking that improves from being made in advance and reheated.

This recipe will make more paste than is needed for the Mussaman curry. However it may be stored in a sealed container for up to 1 week.

The Mussaman curry paste:
2 cardamom pods
1 tbsp coriander seeds
1 tsp cumin seeds
½ tsp grated nutmeg
½ tsp ground cinnamon
½ tsp ground cloves
4 oz/120 g shallots, finely chopped
4 oz/120 g garlic, finely chopped
4 oz/120 g lemon grass, trimmed of all tough leaves, finely sliced into rounds
1 tbsp finely sliced galangal
1 tbsp finely chopped coriander root
1 tsp grated kaffir lime rind
1 tsp ground white pepper
10 large dried red chilies, seeded and roughly chopped
1 tbsp salt

2 tbsp dried shrimp paste

The curry:

4 tbsp vegetable oil

1 garlic clove, finely chopped

10 oz/300 g boneless beef, cut into 1 inch/2.5 cm cubes (lean stewing or flank steak would be excellent)

8 oz/240 g small new potatoes, peeled (they should be about the size of pickling onions)

8 oz/240 g small baby onions, peeled

2 tbsp Mussaman curry paste

8 fl oz/240 ml/1 cup coconut cream (page 178)

8 fl oz/240 ml/1 cup beef stock

3 tbsp/fish sauce

2 tbsp/sugar

2 tbsp tamarind water (page 142)

4 oz/120 g/1 cup roasted peanuts

6 whole cardamom pods

8 cardamom leaves (you may substitute 4 bay leaves)

First make the curry paste. In a wok or frying pan, dry fry the cardamom pods until aromatic. Place in a mortar and pound until powdered. In the same pan, dry fry the coriander and cumin seeds until they are aromatic. Place in the mortar and pound. Add all the other ingredients to the mortar, each in turn, pounding between each addition. When all have been added, pound the whole mixture into a thick paste.

In a wok or frying pan, heat half the oil and fry the garlic until golden brown. Add the beef and continue frying until the juices are sealed in. Remove the beef with a slotted spoon, drain and set aside. Place the potatoes in the hot oil and fry until golden. Remove, drain and set aside. Add the onions to the hot oil and fry until they begin to brown. Remove, drain and set aside. Remove the wok from the heat.

Heat the remaining oil in a large saucepan and fry the curry paste, stirring until it begins to blend. Add the beef and stir well to coat. Add half the coconut cream and bring to the boil, stirring constantly. Add the stock, fish sauce, sugar and tamarind juice and stir as the

liquid returns to the boil. Add the potatoes and stir until boiling again. Add the second half of the coconut cream, the onions, peanuts, cardamom pods and cardamom or bay leaves, and stir well as the mixture returns to the boil. Turn down the heat and simmer for 15 minutes, stirring occasionally.

Test the beef to ensure that it is tender. If not, continue to simmer until you are satisfied. When tender, turn the curry into a bowl and serve.

PORK BELLY WITH FIVE SPICES (F)
—— MOO PA LOW ——

2 tbsp vegetable oil

1 tbsp finely chopped garlic

1 tbsp finely chopped coriander root

2 tbsp five-spice powder

1½ lb/720 g pork belly/fresh side pork, cut into 1 inch/2.5 cm pieces

2 pints/1.2 litres/5 cups chicken stock

2 tbsp dark soy sauce

3 tbsp fish sauce

2 tbsp sugar

fresh coriander leaves/cilantro, to garnish

In a large saucepan, heat the oil and fry the garlic until golden brown. Stirring constantly, add the coriander root and then the five-spice powder. Add the pork and stir-fry until the meat is thoroughly coated with the spices and cooked through. Pour in the stock and bring to the boil, stirring in all the remaining ingredients. Reduce the heat and simmer for 30 minutes. Skim any scum occasionally.

Pour into a bowl, garnish with coriander leaves and serve.

PICKLES AND PRESERVES
KRUEN DONG

Pickling in Thai cooking is used both to preserve ingredients, such as fruits, vegetables, meat and fish, and also to intensify flavours. Pickles can be served as a condiment, as they are in India, Europe and North America, or they can be included in the cooking process as if they were spices.

There are two distinct sorts of pickling – *dong preo,* which could be translated as a sour pickle, and *dong kem* or salty pickle. *Dong preo* consists of pickling ingredients in either salted water or in a mixture of salt, sugar and vinegar. These are 'light' pickles, quickly made and often used as an accompaniment. The ingredient – fruit, vegetable, or whatever – keeps its basic shape. *Dong preo* pickles are easy to make at home and, while they can be bought in jars, it is a pleasure to make one's own, varying the taste to suit oneself.

By contrast, *dong kem* pickles are best left to the expert as they are time consuming and there is very little that the individual cook can add to the final taste. In effect these are not so much pickled as fermented. There are two varieties here, which could be termed 'wet' and 'dry'. The two sorts of 'wet' *dong kem* that you are most likely to encounter are *pla raa,* pickled fish, and *manow dong,* pickled limes. In both cases the ingredient is boiled with large amounts of salt, then cooled and conserved in air-tight containers where it is left for at least a month. The result is tangy fish or lime in a richly flavoured liquid, both of which are used as part of the cooking process. The two 'dry' versions of *dong kem* that occur most often are *chi po,* preserved white radish or mooli/daikon, and *tang chi,* which is made from a variety of hard vegetable stems, though most often from cabbage stems. In both cases the vegetable is mashed with large amounts of salt and left overnight to 'sweat'. The next day the vegetable is kneaded, squeezed dry and left to sun-dry during the day, then returned to the liquid that night. This process is repeated three times until a final sun-drying takes place, after which the dry salty vegetable is sealed into a jar or plastic pack. Only small slivers are needed to enhance the flavour of a dish. *Chi po,* preserved radish, is sold in long pieces and needs to be cut into slivers before use; *tang chi,* preserved vegetable, is already slivered before sealing. Both will keep well in a sealed jar. Some Chinese brands of *chi po* translate it as 'preserved turnip'; this is simply a mistranslation of white radish and not a different product.

▲
Pickled fish, *Pla raa,* made in a large clay jar, neither a pretty sight nor smell, but a deliciously rich and savoury taste.

▶
Pickles and preserves (*Kruen Dong*)

Top shelf: Lime pickle (*Manow dong*); pickled fish (*Pla raa*); preserved vegetable (*Tang chi*). Bottom row: Pickled cabbage (*Pak Gat Dong*); preserved white radish (*Chi po*); pickled garlic (*Kratiam Dong*).

RECIPES
WITH PICKLES AND PRESERVES

CURRIED PORK WITH PICKLED GARLIC (C)
GAENG HAENG LAY

2 tbsp vegetable oil

1 garlic clove, finely chopped

1 tbsp red curry paste (page 89)

4 fl oz/120 ml/½ cup coconut cream (page 178)

4 oz/120 g boneless pork with a little fat, finely slivered

1 inch/2.5 cm piece of fresh ginger, peeled and finely chopped

2 tbsp chicken stock or water

2 tbsp fish sauce

1 tsp sugar

½ tsp turmeric powder

2 tsp lemon juice

4 pickled garlic cloves/*kratiam dong* (page 98), finely chopped

In a wok or frying pan, heat the oil and fry the garlic until golden brown. Add the curry paste and stir in well. Add the coconut cream and stir until the liquid begins to reduce and thicken. Add the pork and stir well to coat. Continue stirring until the pork is cooked through – approximately 1 minute. Add the remaining ingredients in turn, stirring constantly. Turn into a serving bowl and serve.

CHICKEN CURRY NOODLE WITH PICKLED CABBAGE (O)
KOW SOI

This richly flavoured dish shows the influences of our Burmese neighbours who have always had close contacts with the north of Thailand – sadly, often through wars and successive invasions. Happily, this particular arrival is more than welcome, and many people who eat *Kow Soi* become addicted to it. It is ideal on a cold winter's day as it warms up the body and refreshes the sinuses, and leaves you with an all-over glow.

4 oz/120 g fresh *ba mee* noodles, or use 2oz/60 g dry noodles soaked and drained

2 tbsp vegetable oil

1 small garlic clove, finely chopped

1 tsp red curry paste (page 89)

4 fl oz/120 ml/½ cup coconut cream (page 178)

6 oz/180 g boneless chicken, roughly chopped

8 fl oz/240 ml/1 cup chicken stock

1 tsp curry powder

¼ tsp turmeric powder

2 tbsp fish sauce

½ tsp lemon juice

½ tsp sugar

To garnish:

1 spring onion/scallion, coarsely chopped

2 shallots, finely diced

1 tbsp pickled cabbage/*pat gat dong* (opposite)

1 lemon, cut into wedges

Bring a saucepan of water to the boil. Using a sieve or mesh strainer, dip the noodles into the water for a few seconds. Drain and set aside in a serving bowl.

In a wok or frying pan, heat the oil and fry the garlic until golden brown. Add the curry paste and mix in well. Cook for a few seconds. Add the coconut cream, mix in and cook until the liquid starts to reduce and thicken. Add the chicken and stir well, then add the remaining ingredients in turn, stirring constantly.

Pour the chicken mixture over the noodles, put the spring onions, shallots and pickled cabbage on top, and serve with the lemon wedges on the side.

HOT AND SOUR PICKLED CABBAGE (YV)
YAM PAK GAT DONG

This is a recipe for a quick pickle that can be served as a side-dish with curries, but which is also good with less spicy dishes such as fried beef or barbecued meats, where the chili element will 'lift' the taste. It is also useful with rather bland vegetable dishes.

6 oz/180 g pickled cabbage/*Pak Gat Dong* (right)

2 tbsp liquid from the pickled cabbage

2 garlic cloves, finely chopped

4 small fresh red or green chilies, finely chopped

4 shallots, sliced into fine ovals

½ tsp sugar

In a bowl, mix all the ingredients together. Turn into a serving dish.

PICKLED CABBAGE
PAK GAT DONG

You need a firm white cabbage for this pickle. There are several varieties, but the best is a Swatow mustard cabbage, which is available from Chinese shops. It looks rather like a head of lettuce and will already have had the inedible outer blades removed.

1 lb/480 g firm white cabbage, ideally Swatow mustard cabbage, roughly chopped into approximately 2 inch/5 cm square pieces

8 fl oz/240 ml/1 cup rice vinegar

4 oz/120g/9 tbsp sugar

1 tbsp salt

Spread out the chopped cabbage and leave open to the air to dry, until the pieces are just beginning to wilt. In a warm climate or heated room this will take about 24 hours. Then place them in a preserving jar.

In the meantime, bring the vinegar to the boil and dissolve the sugar and salt. Remove from the heat and leave to cool. When cold, pour over the cabbage. Close the jar firmly and leave for 3 days before using – you do not need to refrigerate.

PICKLED GARLIC
━━━━ KRATIAM DONG ━━━━

1 lb/480 g whole garlic cloves (unpeeled)

8 fl oz/240 ml/1 cup rice vinegar

8 oz/240 g/1¼ cups sugar

2 tbsp salt

Place the garlic cloves in a bowl and cover with water. Leave to soak for 1 hour, then drain and pull away the skins. Leave the cloves to dry for about 1 hour.

In the meantime, in a saucepan heat the vinegar and dissolve the sugar and salt. Remove from the heat and leave to cool.

Place the garlic in a preserving jar. Pour over the cold liquid, close tightly and leave for at least 1 month before using.

▲
Night market, selling pickles and preserves.

▶
Chicken Curry Noodle with Pickled Cabbage (*Kow Soi*).

FRIED BEEF WITH PRESERVED RADISH (F)
NUA PAD CHI PO

2 tbsp vegetable oil

2 garlic cloves, finely chopped

8 oz/240 g tender boneless beef, thinly sliced

4 oz/120 g piece of preserved radish/*chi po*, cut crossways to make thin ovals

2 eggs

1 tbsp fish sauce

1 tbsp light soy sauce

1 long fresh red or green chili/*prik chee faa*, cut on the diagonal to make thin ovals

½ tsp sugar

½ tsp ground white pepper

fresh coriander leaves/cilantro, to garnish

In a wok or frying pan, heat the oil and fry the garlic until golden brown. Add the beef and stir well, then add the preserved radish and stir. Break the eggs into the pan and stir gently to coat the beef and the radish with scrambled egg. Before it sets completely, stir in the remaining ingredients. After a final stir, turn on to a serving dish and garnish with coriander leaves.

SPICY PICKLED FISH WITH PRAWN/SHRIMP (D)
PLA RAA SONG KRUEN

This is a spicy dip, a *nam prik*, from the North East. It can be served with raw salad or a selection of vegetables lightly cooked until *al dente*.

4 fl oz/120 ml/½ cup water

4 oz/120 g fish pieces, removed from a jar of pickled fish/*pla raa*, filleted

3 kaffir lime leaves, roughly chopped

1 tbsp finely chopped galangal

1 tbsp finely chopped tender lemon grass

4 shallots, roughly chopped

2 garlic cloves, finely chopped

1 inch/2.5 cm piece of fresh young ginger, peeled and finely sliced into matchsticks

4 or 5 small fresh red or green chilies, finely chopped

4 oz/120 g peeled raw prawns/shrimp, finely chopped

1 tbsp fish sauce

2 tbsp lime juice

1 tsp sugar

Heat the water in a saucepan. Add the pickled fish and simmer, breaking it up, until the liquid begins to thicken. Add all the remaining ingredients, stirring throughout. When the mixture has cooked to a runny paste, turn it into a small bowl. Serve with crudités or cooked vegetables.

DUCK WITH LIME PICKLE (F)
PED TOON MANOW DONG

½ duck, approx 2.5 lb/1.35 kg

1¾ pints/1 litre/4 cups water

vegetable oil for deep frying

20 black peppercorns, slightly crushed

1 pickled lime/*manow dong*

3 garlic gloves, slightly crushed

4 coriander roots, crushed

4 tbsp light soy sauce

½ tsp salt

5 spring onions/scallions, cut into 2 inch/5 cm lengths

Pull the skin and fat from the duck and discard. Remove the meat from the bones and set aside; reserve the bones.

Put the water into a large saucepan and bring to the boil. Add the duck bones and simmer for 30 minutes.

Meanwhile, heat a pan of oil for deep frying to 400°F/200°C. Cut the duck meat into 1½ inch/3.75 cm cubes. Deep fry until golden brown, then drain on paper towels. Add to the simmering stock. Add all the other ingredients and simmer for another 30 minutes.

Remove the bones. Turn the soup into a tureen and serve.

WAN TAN SOUP (S)
GEOW NAM

This is the classic Chinese soup, which has become part of Thai cuisine.

2 garlic cloves, finely chopped

2 oz/60 g minced/ground pork

salt and black pepper

6 wan tan sheets/won ton wrappers

16 fl oz/500 ml/2 cups chicken stock

1 tsp preserved vegetable/*tang chi*

1 tbsp fish sauce

1 tbsp light soy sauce

½ tsp sugar

1 spring onion/scallion, sliced into fine rings

Mix together the garlic, pork, and a sprinkling of salt and pepper. Put an equal portion of this mixture in the centre of each wan tan sheet. Gather up and squeeze the corners together to make a little purse. Set aside.

In a saucepan, heat the stock and add the preserved vegetable. Bring to the boil. Add the wan tan purses together with all the other ingredients except the spring onion. Return to the boil, stirring gently.

Remove from the heat and turn into a tureen. Scatter the spring onion rings and a shaking of pepper on top and serve.

3

FOLLOWING
THE
MEKONG

◆

THE
NORTH-EAST
FROM LAOS
TO CAMBODIA

In July 1966, Stephen Young, a student from Harvard University, was walking through the village of Ban Chiang in north-eastern Thailand where he was conducting anthropological research. Going down a steeply sloping bank, Stephen caught his foot in the root of a kapok tree and was sent sprawling. When he opened his eyes, he saw something smooth and curved sticking out of the ground. Intrigued, he scratched away the earth and uncovered a beautifully fashioned pot – Stephen Young had accidentally stumbled on what may be the world's oldest culture.

Throughout the early 1960s, similar strange vases, with bold russet spiral designs on a sandy background, had been appearing in Bangkok. They were seized upon by discriminating collectors, though no one knew where they came from. Scientists had studied shards of the pottery and the occasional metal tool found with them, and had come up with the seemingly impossible date of 5000 BC, which made them the oldest bronze-age relics ever found. Only when Stephen Young fell down that slope in Ban Chiang, was the secret of their origin revealed.

Since 1966, a series of excavations in and around Ban Chiang has uncovered a wealth of pots – some miraculously intact – and thousands of metal tools. The most highly decorated dishes were grave goods, found beside skeletons, but the more common pots and tool-heads show that these objects were made by a rice-growing people who were practising their skills at least as long ago as, and perhaps even earlier than, the civilizations of Mesopotamia, formerly thought to be the oldest in human history.

Today, Ban Chiang has a handsome museum, set up by Washington's Smithsonian Institution in conjunction with the Department of Fine Arts in Bangkok. These organizations have preserved one of the excavation sites so that visitors can experience some of the same excitement as the archeologists felt, when they brushed away the dust of ages from the bones and jars of this most ancient of peoples.

One of the wider effects of the discovery of the Ban Chiang culture is that it has helped to change common perceptions of Thailand's poorest region. Bangkokians have long looked down on the vast northern province, which they know as Issan after its principle inhabitants. Until recently, few city dwellers and almost no tourists travelled to the region, which was thought to be the back of beyond and which consequently had no decent hotels or good roads. This view was confirmed by years of drought and bad harvests, which drove countless Issan farmers off their land, transforming them into

◄◄
A buffalo at dawn, still the most evocative sight in Asia.

refugees and migrant workers within their own country. Anyone doing hard or dirty work anywhere in Thailand is likely to come from the North-East. Constant trouble along three sides of the region – Laos to the north and east, Cambodia to the south – seemed to confirm Issan's reputation as a difficult and sometimes dangerous place.

Today, these impressions are being radically revised. The construction of the American-Thai Friendship Highway in the 1950s, linking Bangkok to Nong Khai on the bank of the Mekong, almost opposite the Laotian capital Vientiane, began the process of road building and aid projects that is transforming the region. Thai nationals can now cross the Mekong to visit Laos, though foreign visitors must fly into Laos and can only cross back to Nong Khai at the end of their tour. Still, this loosening up looks set to make enormous changes along the border and the first bridge between the two countries has already been completed.

Of course the irony is that there are probably more Laotians in Thailand than in Laos itself, so many having made the crossing to freedom during the worst years of communist repression. Nong Khai is very much an immigrant town, with many of its restaurants being owned by refugees from Vietnam who were allowed to cross into Thailand but forbidden to travel further into the country – thus they had to open businesses near the river. The Vietnamese introduced varieties of charcuterie that were new to Thai cuisine but which are now a firm part of northern cooking.

The best places to eat in Nong Khai are right on the banks of the Mekong, a meandering trickle during the dry season and a broad roaring flood when the rains come. One of the great experiences in Asia is to sit with a drink, watching the sun set over the great curving waters of the Mekong. An ideal place to do this is at the Chai Kong Restaurant – literally 'By-the-Kong-River' – whose cooking is a pleasing mix of Thai, Lao and Vietnamese cuisines.

North-east Thailand, and in particular the area around Nong Khai, has been so little appreciated that few guide books offer an adequate list of what is on offer. For example, you need a local guide to take you to the extraordinary sculpture park that has been developed near the town over the past ten years. It is the work of a solitary, obsessed artist named Loungpou Bounlour Surirat, a Buddhist mystic who has dedicated his life to creating monumental concrete figures based on his fantastic dreams. Although born in Thailand, Bounlour first set up a sculpture park across the border in Laos. He had wanted to be a monk, but when his head was shaved in preparation for ordainment, he went blind; this he took to be a sign that he was meant to use his

vision to create sacred art. When his hair grew back, his sight
returned and he set to work, living the austere life of a monk but
working long hours on his huge sculptures. Driven out of Laos by the
communists, Bounlour began again near Nong Khai, where a number
of prominent citizens helped him to aquire a plot of land. His images
are drawn from the early life of Prince Gautama Buddha and mix
Hindu and Buddhist figures – the Elephant God, Krishna, Rama – all
on a breathtaking scale. Enormous brick structures support the final
concrete layer, moulded on as if it were just a plaster model and not a
massive tower the height of several houses. There is now a line of six
giant Buddhas, each over 65 ft/20 m tall; a mermaid rises to the
height of a two-storey building, and a vast seven-headed dragon, or
Naga, is highest of all, with each of its seven coils standing taller than
a full-grown man.

Perhaps the strangest thing is that there are never any plans or
preliminary sketches for the sculptures. Bounlour insists that he has an
absolutely clear mental image of what he is working towards and
simply starts building up his brick structures as if they were no more
than a child's model, rather than such vast overpowering structures.

Not everyone has been entirely happy with his achievement:
many local people were afraid that the statues harboured evil spirits
and resented his mixing of foreign gods with Thai Bhuddism. Even
Bounlour's austere lifestyle has caused criticism, and at one point he
was jailed for being a communist. Happily, recent years have seen a
gradual acceptance of his unique vision and, now in his seventies, this
unusual mystic/artist is much revered. His sculpture park is certainly
one of the oddest sights in the
region; I doubt anyone would
want to be locked in it at night,
trapped among the looming saints
and demons of one man's vision
of heaven and hell.

Moving from dreams to reality,
the best way to get a complete
picture of this formerly neglected
land is to travel by car along the
northern part of the region, then
down its eastern edge, a journey
that will take you through some of
the least visited areas of Thailand.
If you drive from Nong Khai down
to Udon Thani and across to

◄
The amazing
monumental sculpture
park created by the
mystic artist Loungpou
Bounlour Surirat, near
Nong Khai in north-
eastern Thailand.
(Photograph by the
author.)

▶
Khmer ruins at Phnom
Rung.

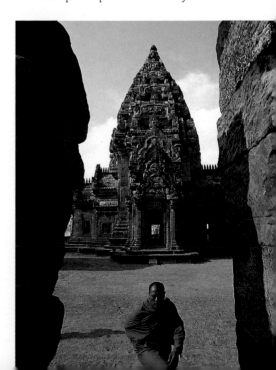

Nakhon Phanom, you again meet up with the Mekong, and can then continue south to Ubon Ratchathani, the last major city before the border with Cambodia.

I recently made this trip during the dry season and was suprised to see neatly banked rice paddies on both sides of the highway, instead of the barren drought-stricken farms I had expected. Improved irrigation and drainage has enabled the farmers to deal with flash-flooding in the rainy season, which used to do much harm. The commonest sight was tobacco leaves – a useful cash crop – spread out on drying frames beside the stilt houses. The wandering buffalo seem fat and contented, gorged on the rice-stubble left from the harvest.

You are more likely to find buffalo meat than beef or other meat in the local cooking, especially in *Laab*, a spicy minced/ground meat dish that includes deep-fried buffalo skin; it is served with a crisp salad of lettuce and mint. As with all poor areas of the world, Issan offers robust, simple peasant cooking that wastes nothing. Thus markets boast frogs, ant grubs, snakes and a much-loved preserve, *pla la,* made from salted river fish and grilled rice, whose pungent aroma spreads everywhere. Wary visitors need not be concerned, however: such things are considered delicacies and are unlikely to be put in front of you unless you specifically ask to try. The best Issan dishes are now well-known all over the country, thanks to cooks like the old woman at the end of our *soi* in Bangkok, making her Issan chicken with *som tam.*

The most remarkable thing about the markets in Issan, was not the oddities but the abundance of the standard ingredients of Thai food. The region has become a major supplier of general foodstuffs. All the basic herbs – mint, basil and coriander – and all the various citrus flavours that provide the essential tangy edge to so many Thai dishes – kaffir limes, lemon grass and tamarind.

I had already eaten a great deal of mint in Nong Khai, as the Vietnamese love the sharp taste of the fresh spearmint leaves in the salads they serve with their delicious spring rolls, and I was to find plenty of lemon grass in the enterprising fish *Laab* I was served on the first stop on my journey in Udon Thani. Two old friends took me to an unprepossessing concrete shop-house restaurant that turned out to have a wonderful cook, Mrs Liew, who came to our table, took our order, and then went off to cook the dishes herself – always the best way to get good original cooking. If you ever venture that far into Thailand, you will find her modest establishment on the Udon Dutsadi Road opposite the Chalerm Wattana Cinema. Make sure to try the wild boar that is first grilled and then quickly stir-fried with green peppercorns.

Driving between Udon Thani and Nakhon Phanom you come
to the turning that leads to the village of Ban Chiang, with its
unmissable excavations and museum. When you meet up with the
Mekong at the end of the day, you can sit by the river sipping a
Mekong whisky, a ferocious spirit, while nibbling on *Si Grot Issan*,
the very garlicky local sausage served with slivers of fresh ginger,
peanuts and finely diced chilies.

Driving down to Ubon, you cannot miss the North-East's most
sacred site, the temple of Wat That Phanom. Its giant *stupa* is 190 ft/
57 m high and is topped with an ornamental parasol made of 35 lb/
16 kg of solid gold. Untold quantities of golden ornaments and
jewellery are said to be embedded within the walls of the soaring
construction. Standing in its shade, it is hard to believe that only
twenty years ago the temple collapsed after four days of unrelenting
monsoon rains. It was restored to its former glory in 1979, but the
catastrophe is a telling reminder of all that the region has had to
suffer from a difficult climate. Even today, the barren fields around
the temple are a vision of what most of Issan was like before all the
recent schemes to ensure a steady supply of water. It is a shock to
finally come out of this rather bleak landscape to find that the city of
Ubon Ratchathani is yet another of Thailand's boom towns, with all
the usual tower blocks and traffic jams.

If you do get as far as Ubon, you should make the extra effort to
see one of the most spectacular sights in South East Asia, the Khmer
temple Khao Phra Viharn. The Khmer were one of the first peoples to
build settlements in what was to become Thailand, radiating
outwards from the heart of their kingdom in what is now Cambodia.
Their greatest achievement was the enormous temple complex of
Angkor Wat. Virtually straight roads spread out from that centre to
distant outposts, miniature versions of the great temple itself, some
of which can still be found in north-east Thailand. The most visited
are Prasat Phnom Rung and Pimai near the city of Korat, which
flourished in the eleventh and twelfth centuries, but are quite modest
compared to the splendours of Khao Phra Viharn, which must have
been a major outstation of Angkor in its heyday.

Visiting the site is far from easy. It used to straddle the border
between Thailand and Cambodia, but in 1963, the World Court
awarded it to Cambodia – a decision that did not alter the fact that
it is easier to reach from the Thai side, given that the temple's three
tiers of prayer halls and shady barrel-vaulted cloisters are perched
some 1670 ft/600 m up the Dongrek mountain range, which has a
sheer drop down on to the plains of Cambodia far, far below.

The site was sealed off throughout much of the bloody civil war in Cambodia, but quite recently an agreement has been patched together. This allows visitors from Thailand to cross over the border to climb up to the ruins – still quite an adventure. You must drive from Ubon to Si Sa Ket and then take a twisting jungle road to the last Thai military post. Having parked your vehicle, there is a fair walk to the little hut where a Cambodian guard in a loose Chinese-style uniform will sell you the ticket that acts as a visa. This permits you to continue down a narrow track, passing more guards who peep out of their concrete pill-boxes as you pass as if you were the enemy. Eventually, you come to the foot of an immense length of stairways and slopes, which stretch on for almost a kilometre, and which will carry you right to the edge of the high cliff overlooking what were once the killing fields of Cambodia. Each succeeding tier of buildings has a larger *gopura* or monumental carved entrance, rich in intertwined sculptural decoration, yet leading to suprisingly intimate inner sanctuaries. The second level is thought to be the best, with splendid carvings of Vishnu in a tale from the Hindu creation myth that dates from the high point of Khmer art in the eleventh century.

The view from the cliff edge is awesome – just to stare down into that benighted country fills the visitor with foreboding. When, only a few months after I was there in 1993, I read that a band of Khmer Rouge guerillas had scaled the cliff and briefly occupied the site, my blood ran cold.

Safely back in Ubon, all one has to worry about is where best to eat and enjoy oneself. The great event of the year is the annual wax candle procession each July, when enormous carved wax effigies, depicting religious and mythical figures, are paraded through the city. After watching the spectacle, the great treat is to head for either Koo Daur Beach or Wat Tai Island on the romantically named Moon River, where you can relax on floating pontoons anchored in the shallows and be served the local specialities: *Nam Prik*, heavy on tomatoes and rather sweet; whole chickens baked on coconut husks in hollows in the sand; *Tom Yam* soup made with lemony tamarind leaves. Families come for picnics. Students skip lectures to spend a lazy afternoon in the shaded floating pavilions, drinking beer and waiting for the cooks who row up in tiny boats to offer fried crab, *Som Tam*, or just boiled peanuts. Lying there, waiting for the next course to drift by, it is hard to accept that the North-East was once a punishment post for Thai civil servants, who felt they were being sent to hell. Today, compared to the pollution and the rat-race in Bangkok, life on the banks of the Moon seems like heaven.

▶
Preparing the elaborate outsize wax candles for Ubon's famous procession which takes place every July.

HERBS
SAMUN PRY

Mint *Bai Saranae*

Mint was rarely used in Thai cooking until the influence of Vietnamese cuisine spread from the North-East where many refugees have settled. The Vietnamese use fresh mint in the salad they serve with *Laab*, the spicy minced/ground meat dish. Mint does not combine well with other herbs, and it is seldom cooked – if it is used in soups it is only 'tossed' in at the last moment before serving, so that it does not dominate all the other flavours. The preferred variety in Thailand is spearmint, with its long oval greyish-green leaves. It has a much stronger flavour than ordinary 'garden' mint. Spearmint grows well in Europe and North America and is easily available. It must always be used fresh and cannot be kept for long – after 24 hours it will begin to wilt. Dried mint is never used in Thai cuisine.

Sweet Basil *Bai Horabha* and **Holy Basil** *Bai Krapow*

Both of these are, in fact, varieties of sweet basil. The herb we call 'sweet' basil is nearest to that much used in Italian cuisine, both raw and cooked. Holy basil, whose leaves are narrower and sometimes have a reddish-purple tinge, has a stronger, more intense taste and must be cooked to release its flavour. There is a third Thai basil, *bai manglak* or lemon-scented basil, which has slightly hairy, paler green leaves. It is delicious but very fragile and cannot be exported easily, so you are unlikely to find it outside Thailand. The more robust sweet and holy basils can be dried and do not have to be soaked before using. While some of the flavour will be lost in the drying process, it is the only way to preserve basil as the delicate leaves are damaged if frozen.

Coriander *Pak Chee*

Coriander is also known as cilantro or Chinese parsley – it is, indeed, a member of the parsley family and much resembles flat-leaf or Italian parsley. Like its relation, coriander leaves are generally used as a garnish in Thai cooking, whole or chopped up and scattered on a finished dish, as much for the visual effect as the flavour. The seeds, which have quite a different taste, are used as a spice; they are dealt with on page 86.

Coriander root is much used in Thai cooking – some dishes require a great many roots and this often creates a problem in the West where suppliers tend to chop off the root. The only solutions are to persuade your greengrocer to get some uncut coriander or for you to look for any bunches that have one or two roots still surviving. Cut off the roots with about ¼ inch/5 mm of the stalk, wash them carefully and freeze them to be used as needed. Although a little wet on thawing, they are perfectly adequate. If you cannot get any roots then just use an extra length of the lower stalks. Coriander leaves are now so easy to obtain that preservation is hardly necessary – the washed plant will keep for a few days in a refrigerator, either wrapped in a plastic bag or in a salad compartment.

BEEF NOODLE SOUP WITH MINT LEAVES (O)

—— GUEYTEOW NUA SOT BAI SARANAE ——

2 tbsp vegetable oil

2 garlic cloves, finely chopped

2 oz/60 g/½ cup fresh beansprouts

2 oz/40 g *sen lek* noodles, soaked and drained

4 oz/120 g boneless tender beef, finely slivered

20 fresh mint leaves

The soup:

16 fl oz/500 ml/2 cups beef stock

1 cinnamon stick

2 star anise

2 tbsp fish sauce

1 tbsp light soy sauce

1 tsp sugar

½ tsp ground white pepper

First, put all the soup ingredients into a large saucepan and bring to the boil. Turn down the heat and simmer for 15 minutes.

In the meantime, heat the oil in a small pan and fry the garlic until golden brown. Set aside.

Heat a saucepan of water until it boils. Using a mesh sieve or strainer, plunge in the beansprouts. Remove and drain, then turn into a serving bowl. Next, plunge in the noodles in the sieve, leave for 10 seconds and then remove and drain. Add to the serving bowl. Plunge in the beef and boil until just cooked through. Drain, and turn into the bowl.

Pour the garlic and oil into the bowl and thoroughly stir together the beef, noodles and beansprouts. Scatter the mint leaves into the bowl, then pour in the soup. Serve immediately.

PRAWN/SHRIMP CURRY WITH SWEET BASIL (C)

—— PENANG GUNG ——

2 tbsp vegetable oil

2 garlic cloves, finely chopped

1 tbsp red curry paste (page 89)

6 oz/180 g raw prawns/shrimp, peeled and de-veined

4 fl oz/120 ml/½ cup coconut cream (page 178)

1 tbsp ground roasted peanuts

20 fresh sweet basil leaves

1 long fresh red chili/*prik chee faa*, finely slivered lengthways

2 kaffir lime leaves, rolled up into a cigarette shape and finely slivered across

In a wok or frying pan, heat the oil and fry the garlic until it begins to brown. Add the curry paste and stir it in well. Add the remaining ingredients in turn, except the chili and lime leaves, stirring well between each addition. Stir-fry until the prawns are cooked through. Turn on to a serving dish and garnish with the slivered chili and kaffir lime leaves.

BEEF WITH HOLY BASIL (F)

—————— **NUA PAD KRAPOW** ——————

2 tbsp oil
2 garlic cloves, finely chopped
2 small fresh red or green chilies, finely chopped
6 oz/180 g lean minced/ground beef
1 medium-size onion, halved and roughly sliced
2 tbsp fish sauce
1 tbsp light soy sauce
1 tsp sugar
20 fresh holy basil leaves

In a wok or frying pan, heat the oil and fry the garlic and chilies, stirring well, until the garlic begins to brown. Add the minced/ground beef and stir-fry, breaking apart the meat and mixing in the garlic and chili. Add the remaining ingredients, mixing well. Stir-fry until the beef is cooked through. Turn on to a dish and serve.

◀

Herbs (*Samun Pry*)
From left: Coriander
(*pak chee*); sweet basil
(*bai horabha*); mint (*bai
saranae*); holy basil (*bai
krapow*).

GRILLED CHICKEN WITH CORIANDER SAUCE (F)
GAI YANG

14 oz/420 g boneless chicken breasts, with skin
2 tbsp sesame oil
2 garlic cloves, finely chopped
1 tsp finely chopped coriander root
2 small fresh red chilies, finely chopped
2 tbsp fish sauce
1 tsp sugar
The sauce:
6 tbsp rice vinegar
4 tbsp sugar
½ tsp salt
2 garlic cloves, finely chopped
1 tbsp finely chopped coriander/cilantro (leaf and stalk)
5 small fresh red chilies, finely chopped

In a large bowl, mix the chicken breasts with all the other ingredients. Leave to marinate for 30 minutes.

Meanwhile, make the sauce. In a small saucepan, heat the vinegar, add the sugar and stir until dissolved. Add the salt and simmer, stirring, until the liquid thickens. Remove from the heat and allow to cool. Add the remaining sauce ingredients, stir well and turn into a small bowl.

Preheat the grill/broiler. Cook the marinated chicken under the grill, turning as necessary. Serve with the sauce.

ISSAN SAUSAGE (H)
SI GROT ISSAN

For this recipe you will need to find a butcher able to supply you with sausage skins – not an easy task these days. Because I make a great deal of sausage for my restaurant I buy skins in bulk from a supplier, but I remember how difficult it was when I was starting out and only needed to find a small amount. There is an artificial substitute for pig's intestines, which can be used as a sausage skin, but I have never actually seen it. You will just have to persevere, preferably by tracking down an old-fashioned butcher who can advise you.

2 tsp finely chopped coriander root
8 oz/240 g pork belly with fat/fresh pork side, minced/ground
1 lb/480 g/2½ cups cooked sticky rice
4 oz/120 g garlic, finely chopped
1 tsp salt

In a bowl, mix all the ingredients together, preferably kneading with your fingers. Put a funnel into one end of the tube of sausage skin and tie a knot in the opposite end. Force in about a 3 inch/7.5 cm length of the meat mixture and knead it down to the knotted end. When it is firmly packed in, tie a knot in the tube. Repeat the process until all the meat mixture is used and the tube is a string of sausages.

Hang the string to dry – you can cook the sausages after 1 day, but if you want a mature 'sour' taste leave them for 48 hours.

The sausages can be grilled/broiled, either in the entire string or individually, skewered on brochettes. You can test that they are cooked by pricking with a fork, if no fat bubbles out when the fork is removed then the process is complete. Or deep fry them, pricking the skin in several places before plunging them into the hot oil.

Serve with sprigs of fresh coriander/cilantro, fine slivers of fresh ginger, roasted peanuts and finely chopped small fresh red or green chilies.

STEAMED MUSHROOM CURRY WITH SWEET BASIL (TV)
MUK HET

In Thailand we would make little banana leaf cups in which to steam this curry. They impart a slight flavour to the final dish but as there is usually great difficulty in getting such leaves I have suggested you use small ramekin dishes instead. You could, of course, use any small heatproof bowls or even cups. Because these containers vary in thickness it is impossible to give an exact time for the steaming process, so I suggest that you check by pricking with a fork; it should come out without any trace of liquid once cooking is completed.

2 oz/60 g/4½ tbsp sticky rice, soaked in cold water for 2 hours
8 oz/240 g fresh oyster mushrooms, roughly sliced crossways
2 tbsp red curry paste (page 89)
2 tbsp light soy sauce
1 tsp sugar
1 egg
20 fresh sweet basil leaves
1 long fresh red chili/*prik chee faa*, finely slivered lengthways

Drain the sticky rice, place in a mortar and pound briefly to crush slightly. Put the crushed rice grains into a large mixing bowl and add the mushrooms, red curry paste, soy sauce and sugar. Break the egg into the bowl and stir thoroughly.

Take 2 ramekins and place 10 sweet basil leaves at the bottom of each. Pour in the rice mixture and sprinkle the slivered chili on top. Bring water to the boil in the bottom part of a steamer. Place the ramekins in the top part, cover and steam for about 30 minutes.

HOT BASIL SOUP (S)
CAENG KRAPOW

This is a basic soup to which various ingredients can be added. I've chosen fish balls, but you could use beef balls or small pieces of meat, fish or prawns, cooking a little longer depending on what you are using. This is quite a fiery dish, and good if you've got a cold. Add more chili if you really want to clear you sinuses!

16 fl oz/480 ml/2 cups chicken stock
1 tbsp fish sauce
1 tbsp light soy sauce
4 oz/120 g medium-size onion, sliced into thin rounds, then finely slivered
6 oz/180 g fish balls (see page 74)
15 holy basil leaves
1 small fresh red or green chilli/*prik khee noo*, finely chopped

In a saucepan, bring the stock gently to the boil and while simmering stir in all the ingredients except the basil. Cook for 5 seconds, remove from the heat, add the basil and chili and pour at once into a tureen and serve.

BAMBOO SHOOTS
NORMAI

For those who are only familiar with bamboo as a tall, hard, stick-like plant – either used decoratively in gardens and pots, or usefully in furniture – it is usually a shock to realize that throughout Asia it is an edible plant. The key word here is 'shoot', for it is the first stage of the bamboo as it appears out of the ground that is eaten. The fresh bamboo shoot is ivory white after being stripped of its fine, needle-sharp hairs. It must be parboiled before use, to remove the bitter, poisonous hydrocyanic acid it contains. That done, the shoot can then be sliced and used as a vegetable in salads and stir-fries. It is, however, unlikely that Western cooks will be involved in this process. Even in Thailand it is usually only village people who use fresh shoots – city dwellers mainly buy ready parboiled shoots in food markets. Outside Thailand bamboo shoots are normally bought canned and thus already parboiled.

There are several varieties of bamboo shoots, though they are usually just divided into spring shoots and winter shoots, with the latter being considered the most tender and sweet. Unfortunately, cans of bamboo shoots do not specify which variety is contained within, so the difference is purely academic in the West. Canned in brine, the shoots are usually yellowish in colour. Once opened, they can be kept in water, in a closed container, in the refrigerator for several days.

Bamboo shoots have a low calorie content and they are rich in vitamin B and phosphorous. No medicinal properties are ascribed to the plant. On the contrary, many Thais have a superstitious belief that if you eat the plant while you are unwell it delays recovery.

In cooking, bamboo shoots are appreciated for their hard texture, which contrasts well with softer vegetables, especially in soups and curries. Because it is one of the few oriental vegetables that is normally canned, it is a useful emergency stand-by when an instant meal is needed.

◀
Backstage at an open-air puppet show, a popular feature at village fairs and celebrations.

▶
Various forms of tinned bamboo shoots: large sliced, thin whole and ready shredded.

RECIPES
WITH BAMBOO SHOOTS

HOT AND SOUR VERMICELLI SOUP (SV)
RANG NOK TIAM

4 dried Chinese mushrooms

6 oz/180 g *wun sen* noodles

1½ pints/900 ml/3¾ cups vegetable stock

4 oz/120 g/½ cup bamboo shoots, finely sliced into matchsticks

6 tbsp light soy sauce

1 tbsp sugar

1 tsp cornflour/cornstarch, mixed with a little water

1 small spring onion/scallion, finely sliced

fresh coriander leaves/cilantro, to garnish

The condiment:

4 small fresh red or green chilies, finely chopped

6 tbsp rice vinegar

Soak the mushrooms in cold water for 1 hour; drain and set aside. At the same time, soak the noodles for 1 hour; drain and set aside.

For the condiment, mix the chilies with the vinegar in a small bowl. Set aside.

In a large saucepan, bring the stock to the boil. Add the mushrooms, noodles, bamboo shoots, soy sauce and sugar and bring back to the boil. Stir in the cornflour mixture. Simmer for 2 minutes or until thickened.

Pour into a tureen and garnish with spring onion and coriander leaves. Serve with the condiment.

MINCED BEEF FRIED WITH BAMBOO SHOOTS (F)
NUA SAB NORMAI

2 tbsp sesame oil

2 garlic cloves, finely chopped

6 oz/180 g minced/ground beef

3 oz/90 g/⅓ cup bamboo shoots, diced into tiny cubes

2 oz/60 g/¼ cup waterchestnuts, diced into tiny cubes

½ tsp chili powder

1 tbsp fish sauce

1 tbsp light soy sauce

1 tsp sugar

lettuce leaves, to serve

In a wok or frying pan, heat the oil and fry the garlic until golden brown. Add the beef and stir-fry until cooked through and crumbly. Add all the remaining ingredients in turn, stirring constantly.

Turn on to a serving dish. Serve with the lettuce leaves, which are used as envelopes to wrap round a mouthful of the beef mixture.

CHICKEN CURRY WITH BAMBOO SHOOTS (C)
GAENG NORMAI GAI

4 fl oz/120 ml/½ cup coconut cream (page 178)

2 tbsp vegetable oil

1 garlic clove, finely chopped

1 tbsp red curry paste (page 89)

2 tbsp fish sauce

1 tsp sugar

6 oz/180 g boneless chicken breast, finely sliced

4 fl oz/120 ml/½ cup chicken stock

2 kaffir lime leaves, roughly chopped

4 oz/120 g/½ cup bamboo shoot, cut into slivers

20 fresh holy basil leaves

In a small pan, gently heat the coconut cream but do not let it boil. In a wok or frying pan, heat the oil and fry the garlic until golden brown. Add the curry paste and stir well. Pour in the warmed coconut cream and stir until it begins to reduce and thicken. Add the fish sauce and sugar and stir. Add the chicken and cook, stirring constantly, until the meat is opaque. Add the stock, stir and cook for 1–2 minutes or until the chicken is cooked through. Stir in the lime leaves, then add the bamboo shoot and basil leaves. Stir and cook gently for a final minute. Turn into a serving dish.

PRAWN/SHRIMP CURRY WITH BAMBOO SHOOTS (C)
GAENG KUWA NORMAI

2 tbsp vegetable oil
1 large garlic clove, finely chopped
1 tbsp red curry paste (page 89)
8 fl oz/240 ml/1 cup coconut milk (page 178)
2 tbsp fish sauce
1 tsp sugar
12 large raw prawns/shrimp, peeled and de-veined
4oz/120g/½ cup bamboo shoots, cut into slivers
2 kaffir lime leaves, finely sliced
1 small fresh red chilli, slivered lengthways
10 fresh holy basil leaves

In a wok or frying pan, heat the oil and fry the garlic until golden brown. Add the curry paste and cook briefly, stirring well. Stir in half the coconut milk, the fish sauce and the sugar. Add the prawns and bamboo shoot and cook until they become opaque. Add the remaining coconut milk, the lime leaves and the chilies. Stir and cook until the prawns are cooked through.

With a slotted spoon or sieve, lift out the prawns and arrange them on a serving dish. Add the basil leaves to the sauce and stir briefly, then pour over the prawns and serve.

HOT AND SOUR BAMBOO SALAD (YV)
SUP NORMAI

3 tbsp vegetable stock
2 tbsp light soy sauce
1 tbsp lemon juice
½ tsp sugar
1 tsp chili powder
6 oz/180 g/¾ cup bamboo shoot, shredded
1 tbsp pounded dry-fried rice (page 24)
1 small spring onion/scallion, finely chopped
fresh coriander leaves/cilantro, to garnish

In a saucepan, heat together the stock, soy sauce, lemon juice, sugar and chili powder. Bring quickly to the boil, then add the shredded bamboo shoot and stir thoroughly. Add the dry-fried rice, stir and turn on to a serving dish. Garnish with the spring onion and coriander leaves and serve.

PORK FRIED WITH EGG AND BAMBOO SHOOTS (F)
NORMAI PAD KAI

2 tbsp vegetable oil
1 garlic clove, finely chopped
6 oz/180 g boneless lean pork, finely sliced
1 egg
2 oz/60 g/¼ cup bamboo shoots, roughly sliced
2 oz/60 g canned straw mushrooms, halved
2 tbsp light soy sauce
1 tbsp fish sauce
½ tsp sugar
½ tsp ground white pepper
2 spring onions/scallions, finely chopped

In a wok or frying pan, heat the oil and fry the garlic until golden brown. Add the pork and stir until the meat starts to turn white. Break the egg into the pan and mix thoroughly. Stirring constantly, add the remaining ingredients in turn except the spring onions. Continue stir-frying until the meat is cooked through. At the last moment, stir in the spring onions and turn on to a serving dish.

LIME, KAFFIR LIME AND KAFFIR LIME LEAF

MANAO, MAGRUT, BAI MAGRUT

From a cook's point of view, the essential difference between the light green lime, familiar in the West, and the darker, knobbly kaffir, or wild, lime, is juice – the kaffir lime doesn't have any. While all of a lime, rind and juice, can be used, only the rind of the kaffir lime is serviceable. The reason kaffir lime is so much liked in Thailand is that its rind has a much more intense and zesty flavour than its lighter cousin. Indeed, we tend to think that there is little difference between a lemon and an ordinary lime (we use the same word, *manao*, for both). You can peel a kaffir lime and freeze the rind for future use.

We also use the leaves of the kaffir lime as a herb. They are much appreciated for the pungent lemony aroma they give to a dish. They too can be frozen or allowed to dry, and are used much as bay leaves are in the West. Unless otherwise specified, the kaffir lime leaves in the recipes in this book are fresh. Where dry leaves are used they need not be soaked but can be put straight into the mixture in the same way as bay leaves.

▶
Kaffir lime leaf (*bai magrut*) kaffir lime (*magrut*) and lime (*manao*).

▼
Whole suckling pig, flambéed traditional style.

RECILPES

WITH LIME, KAFFIR LIME, AND KAFFIR LIME LEAF

HOT AND SOUR CRISPY SQUID AND LIME SALAD (Y)
YAM PLA MUK GROB

1 small lime
vegetable oil for deep frying
7 oz/210 g cleaned baby squid, sliced into rings
30 fresh sweet basil leaves
2 stalks of lemon grass, trimmed of all tough leaves, finely chopped into rings
10 kaffir lime leaves, rolled up into a cigarette shape and finely sliced across
4 oz/120 ml/1 cup roasted peanuts
5 small fresh red or green chilies, finely chopped
½ tsp salt

Cut the lime into quarters. Remove and discard the core and most of the seeds. Dice the segments, with the skin, to make tiny cubes, removing any remaining seeds. Set aside.

Heat a pan of oil for deep frying to 400°F/200°C. Using a mesh sieve or strainer, deep fry the squid until golden and crispy. Drain on paper towels and turn into a large mixing bowl. Deep fry the basil until crispy; drain and turn into the bowl. Repeat the process with the lemon grass and then the kaffir lime leaves.

Add all the remaining ingredients, including the reserved lime cubes, to the bowl. Mix well, then turn on to a plate and serve.

FISH CAKES WITH KAFFIR LIME LEAF (H)
TOD MAN PLA

This recipe makes 20 cakes.

5 dried red chilies, halved and seeded
1 shallot, finely sliced
2 garlic cloves, roughly chopped
2 coriander roots, chopped
1 tbsp finely chopped galangal
6 kaffir lime leaves, finely chopped
½ tsp salt
1 lb/480 g ground/minced white fish fillet (cod, coley, haddock or monkfish)
1 tbsp fish sauce
2 oz/60 g thin green beans, sliced very fine
vegetable oil for deep frying
The cucumber relish:
4 fl oz/120 ml/½ cup rice vinegar
2 tbsp sugar
2 inch/5 cm piece of English cucumber, (unpeeled)
1 small carrot
3 shallots, finely sliced
1 medium-size fresh red chili, finely sliced
1 tbsp ground roasted peanuts

For the relish, heat the vinegar with the sugar, stirring until it dissolves, then boil until a thin syrup is formed (6–7 minutes). Quarter the cucumber lengthways, then slice across finely. Halve the carrot lengthways and slice across finely. Add the cucumber, carrot, shallots and chili to the syrup once it is cool and mix thoroughly. Set aside.

In a mortar, pound the chilies, shallot, garlic, coriander roots, galangal, kaffir lime leaves and salt to form a paste. Place the paste in a mixing bowl and, using your fingers, thoroughly blend with the fish. Add the fish sauce and the green beans and knead together. Shape into small flat cakes about 2 inches/5 cm across and about ½ inch/1.25 cm thick.

Heat a pan of oil for deep frying to 400°F/200°C. Deep fry the cakes until golden brown on both sides. The frying time should be between 2 and 3 minutes. Drain on paper towels.

Sprinkle the ground peanuts on top of the relish, stir once, and serve with the fish cakes.

BEEF WITH KAFFIR LIME LEAF AND HOT CHILI (F)
— NUA MOW —

2 tbsp vegetable oil
2 garlic cloves, finely chopped
3 small fresh red chilies, finely chopped
8 oz/240 g tender boneless beef, finely sliced
1 tbsp fish sauce
1 tbsp light soy sauce
1 tbsp oyster sauce
½ tsp sugar
5 kaffir lime leaves, rolled up into a cigarette shape and finely sliced across
1 medium-size onion, roughly chopped

In a wok or frying pan, heat the oil and fry the garlic until golden brown. Stirring constantly, add each remaining ingredient in turn. Continue stir-frying until the beef is cooked through, then turn on to a dish and serve.

RARE BEEF WITH LIME (H)
— NUA YANG MANAO —

8 oz/240 g sirloin steak, cut ½ inch/1.25 cm thick, with a little trimming of fat
1 large garlic clove
5 small fresh red or green chilies/*prik kee noo*
4 oz/120 g long bean, cut into 2 inch/5 cm pieces
1 medium-size tomato, cut into wedges
2 tbsp fish sauce
1 tbsp sugar
2 tbsp lime juice
1 tsp finely slivered lime peel

Put the whole steak under a very hot grill/broiler and cook briefly until both sides are well browned, but the centre remains rare. Remove, cut into thin slices and set aside.

In a large mortar, pound the garlic with the chilies until well mashed. Add the long beans and pound briefly so that they are just broken. Add the tomatoes and pound briefly, then stir in the slices of rare beef along with any juices. Add all the remaining ingredients, stirring well. Turn on to a plate and serve.

▶▶
Upper left: Fish Cakes with Kaffir Lime Leaf (*Tod Man Pla*), with cucumber relish. Upper right: Grilled Chicken with Coriander Sauce (*Gai Yang*). Bottom front: Hot and Sour Bamboo Salad (*Sup Normai*).

CHICKEN WITH LIME (F)
GAI MANAO

2 tbsp vegetable oil

2 garlic cloves, finely chopped

8 oz/240 g boneless chicken breast, roughly chopped

1 tbsp finely chopped fresh ginger

1 tbsp black bean sauce, drained to remove excess salted water

½ lime, sliced into thin rounds

2 tbsp lime juice

1 tbsp light soy sauce

½ tsp sugar

½ tsp chili powder

4 thin slivers of lime peel

In a wok or frying pan, heat the oil and fry the garlic until golden brown. Stirring constantly, add each remaining ingredient in turn. Continue stir-frying until the chicken is cooked through. Turn on to a dish and serve.

PORK RIND IN LIME DRESSING (H)
NAM SOT

This snack is usually served with drinks before a main meal. You will need pork rind or skin with no meat and barely any fat – if you cannot get your butcher to supply it you will have to cut it carefully away from a fresh piece of pork, such as a leg roast.

6 oz/180 g piece of pork skin or rind

5 small fresh red or green chilies/*prik kee noo*, finely chopped

1 garlic clove, sliced into ovals

2 tbsp lime juice

6 oz/180 g minced/ground pork

2 tbsp fish sauce

2 tbsp fresh ginger, finely slivered into very thin matchsticks

6 large shallots, thinly sliced into ovals

2 tsp sugar

2 oz/60 g/½ cup roasted peanuts

2 spring onions/scallions, finely chopped

crisp lettuce, to serve

fresh coriander leaves/cilantro, to garnish

Blanch the whole piece of pork skin in boiling water for 15 minutes. Meanwhile, in a small bowl, soak the chilies and the garlic in the lime juice. Drain the pork skin and slice into thin strips about 2 inches/5 cm long.

In a small saucepan over a moderate heat, stir together the minced/ground pork and the fish sauce until the meat separates and becomes pale. Continue stirring until the pork is just cooked but still remains whitish in colour – about 5 minutes. Remove the pan from the heat

Place the sliced pork skin in the saucepan and mix well. Add the ginger, shallots, sugar, peanuts and spring onion and stir well. Pour in the lime juice mixture and mix well.

Arrange lettuce leaves around a serving platter. Place the pork mixture in the centre. Garnish with coriander leaves and serve. The lettuce is used as a scoop to carry the mixture.

GRILLED FISH WITH KAFFIR LIME LEAVES (F)
PLA POW BI MAGRUT

In Thailand this dish is made with river fish. Because the fish is grilled/broiled it must have a firm flesh. Trout would be excellent.

2 garlic cloves, peeled
½ tsp black peppercorns
4 kaffir lime leaves, finely chopped
1 medium-size trout or similar, firm-fleshed fish, cleaned
The sauce:
4 large fresh red chilies, roughly chopped
5 shallots, peeled
5 garlic cloves, peeled
2 tbsp lime juice
2 tbsp fish sauce
1 tbsp sugar

Preheat the grill/broiler.

For the sauce, place the chilies, shallots and garlic in a foil envelope and heat under the grill until there is a slight smell of charring and vegetables feel soft. Unwrap the grilled vegetables and place in a mortar. Pound together. Add the lime juice, fish sauce and sugar and stir well. Turn into a small bowl and set aside.

In the mortar, pound the garlic, then add the peppercorns and pound together. Mix in the kaffir lime leaves. Stuff the mixture inside the fish.

Grill/broil the fish until cooked through, turning once. Place on a dish and serve with the sauce.

PORK CURRY WITH MORNING GLORY/WATER SPINACH AND KAFFIR LIME (C)
MOO TE PO

2 tbsp vegetable oil
2 garlic cloves, finely chopped
1 tbsp red curry paste (page 89)
8 fl oz/240 ml/1 cup coconut milk (page 178)
8 oz/240 g boneless lean pork, roughly chopped
1 small kaffir lime, halfed
4 kaffir lime leaves, roughly chopped
1 tbsp fish sauce
1 tbsp light soy sauce
1 tbsp tamarind water (page 142)
1 tsp sugar
8 fl oz/240 ml/1 cup chicken stock
4 oz/120 g morning glory/water spinach (page 37), roughly chopped into 2 inch/5 cm lengths

In a large saucepan, heat the oil and fry the garlic until golden brown. Stir in the curry paste and cook for a few seconds, then add the coconut milk and stir in well. Cook until it begins to reduce and thicken. Stirring constantly, add all the remaining ingredients, except the stock and morning glory. Continue stirring until the pork is opaque.

Add the stock and bring to the boil. Add the morning glory and simmer for 5 minutes or until it is cooked *al dente*. Turn into a bowl and serve.

LEMON GRASS
TAKRAI

In its natural state, lemon grass is exactly that –
a grass, easily recognized by its long, lemony-
smelling blades. In warm climates, it grows
quickly and abundantly, one stalk multiplying
to almost fifty in a single season. It will
occasionally produce a flower, but even in
Thailand this is rare.

Lemon grass is found throughout South East
Asia, India, Central and Southern America and
the West Indies. It can be cultivated under hot-
house conditions in temperate climates but
needs great care. The main lemon-grass
growing areas in Thailand are around the cities
of Nakhon Ratchasima (Korat) in the East,
Kamphang Phet in the Central Plains and
Samut Prakharn near Bangkok.

When you find it in a market, the grassy
leaves will have been chopped off. What
remains is the lower stalk from which the
coarsest outer leaves will have been stripped.
The pale green, almost white, bulbous stalk
now looks something like a fat spring
onion/scallion or a small leek.

◄

Meat is usually very
fresh in Thailand, but
butchers are only rarely
Thai – the task is most
often left to Muslims or
non-Bhuddist Chinese.

▶

Lemon Grass (*Takrai*)

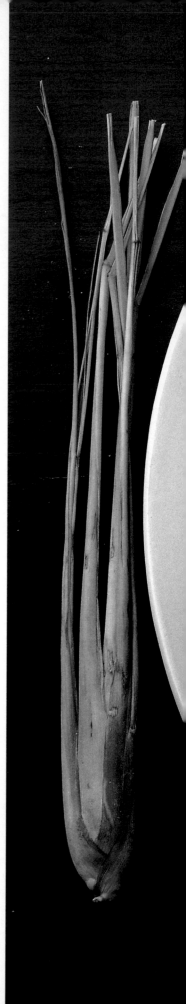

When first bought, there is no smell, but crush or snap the stalk and it will give off a refreshing aroma of lemon with a hint of mint. Little wonder that in Thailand lemon grass is also used like smelling salts and is thought to be good for headaches. Its other traditional uses are in perfume or in lemon-grass 'tea', which is a good remedy for lack of appetite, fever and gall-stones. It is certainly rich in vitamin A.

When cooked, lemon grass imparts a fresh citrus taste, unlike the acidity of lemon, with a hint of ginger. It is this combination that is unique to the plant and which cannot be exactly reproduced from any other source.

The stalk is roughly 9 inches/23 cm long. There are two ways to use it.

1 Cut the stalk across into several roughly equal pieces. Break them open by crushing slightly with a pestle, flat of a large knife or the back of a wooden spoon. Use to flavour soups and other liquid dishes. The pieces should, like bay leaves, be removed before serving; or the diners should be advised not to eat the lemon grass as it will be hard and stringy.

2 Strip away any tough outer leaves and finely slice the remaining tender stalk into tiny rings. These can be cooked and eaten, even in a stir-fry, provided that only the most tender part of the stalk has been used.

Fine rings of fresh lemon grass can be frozen and stored almost indefinitely; there is no need to thaw before use. Fresh lemon grass is now easily obtainable in the West, but if you do not have access to a supply, oriental and Indian stores also sell powdered lemon grass and should supply this through mail-order. Another substitute is grated lemon zest with a tiny sprinkling of ground ginger, but only as a last resort.

CHICKEN WITH LEMON GRASS CURRY (C)
OOK GAI

3 tbsp vegetable oil

2 garlic cloves, finely chopped

12 oz/350 g chicken on the bone, breast or thigh, roughly chopped into small pieces

3 tbsp fish sauce

4 fl oz/120 ml/½ cup chicken stock

1 tsp sugar

1 stalk of lemon grass, chopped into 4 pieces and slightly crushed

5 kaffir lime leaves, rolled up into a cigarette shape and finely sliced across

The curry paste:

1 stalk of lemon grass, trimmed of all tough leaves, coarsely chopped

1 inch/2.5 cm piece of galangal, peeled and coarsely chopped

2 kaffir lime leaves, chopped

3 shallots, coarsely chopped

6 coriander roots, coarsely chopped

2 garlic cloves

4 long dried red chilies/*prik chee faa haeng*, seeded and coarsely chopped

1 tsp dried shrimp paste

1 tsp turmeric powder

For the curry paste, in a mortar, pound all the ingredients together well. Set aside.

In a wok or frying pan, heat the oil and fry the garlic until golden brown. Add the curry paste and stir well, then cook briefly. Add the chicken pieces and stir until thoroughly coated with the paste. Add the fish sauce, stock and sugar and stir well. Add the lemon grass and lime leaves and stir. Lower the heat and gently simmer for 15 minutes. If the mixture begins to dry out, add a little more stock or water, though not too much as the final curry should be fairly dry. Remove the lemon grass stalks or warn diners not to eat them.

Turn on to a serving dish and serve.

HOT AND SOUR SOUP WITH PRAWNS/SHRIMP AND LEMON GRASS (S)
TOM YAM GUNG

Tom yam is a basic method of making soup and you can use it with various ingredients other than prawns – mussels, scallops, crab claws, chicken pieces or thinly sliced beef.

16 fl oz/500 ml/2 cups chicken stock
1 tbsp *tom yam* sauce (page 84)
2 kaffir lime leaves, finely chopped
2 in/5 cm piece of tender lemon grass, roughly chopped
3 tbsp lemon juice
3 tbsp fish sauce
1–2 small fresh red or green chilies, finely chopped
½ tsp sugar
8 straw mushrooms, halved (canned mushrooms will do)
8 oz/240 g small raw prawns/shrimp, peeled and de-veined

In a saucepan, heat the stock and the *tom yam* sauce. Add the lime leaves, lemon grass, lemon juice, fish sauce, chilies and sugar. Bring to the boil and simmer for 2 minutes. Add the mushrooms and prawns, stir and cook for a further 2–3 minutes or until the prawns are cooked through. Turn into soup bowls and serve.

CRISPY LEMON GRASS WITH BEANCURD (FV)
CHOO CHEE TAKRAI

4 oz/120 g ready-fried beancurd, cut into small cubes
oil for deep frying
2 tbsp oil
2 in/5 cm piece of lemon grass, finely chopped into rings
2 oz/60 g broccoli stems, cut diagonally into 1 in/2.5 cm lengths
2 oz/60 g long beans, chopped into 1 in/2.5 cm lengths
2 oz/60 g baby sweetcorn
2 oz/60 g mangetout/snow peas
3 tbsp vegetable stock
2 tbsp light soy sauce
½ tsp sugar
The paste:
2 large dry red chilies/*prik chee faa haeng*, roughly chopped
2 in/5 cm piece of lemon grass, finely chopped
4 small shallots, finely chopped

To make the paste, pound all the ingredients together in a mortar until a paste forms. Set aside.

Deep fry the beancurd cubes in oil until crispy. Drain and set aside.

In a wok or frying pan, heat the 2 tbsp oil and fry the lemon grass until golden brown and crispy. Stir in the reserved paste, followed by the broccoli, long beans, sweetcorn and mangetout/snow peas. Stir well.

Add the beancurd, stirring continuously, then add the stock, soy sauce and sugar. Make sure everything is mixed in well, then turn on to a warmed plate and serve.

134

HOT AND SOUR SALAD WITH CRAB AND LEMON GRASS (Y)
PLAA POO

This will provide enough for 2 people.

1 large live crab, weighing about 2 lb/900 g
2 tbsp lime juice
2 tbsp fish sauce
1 tsp sugar
½ tsp chili powder
1 tbsp finely chopped tender lemon grass
3 shallots, finely chopped
2 kaffir lime leaves, finely chopped
2 spring onions/scallions, finely chopped

Kill the crab (or have your fishmonger do this for you). With a large kitchen chopper, separate the shell from the body. Crack the claws and chop the body into quarters. Scrape out and discard any inedible parts. Bring water to the boil in the bottom of a steamer.

Place the crab pieces on a heatproof plate and put into the top part of the steamer. Cover and steam for 10 minutes.

In the meantime, in a bowl, thoroughly mix all the other ingredients. When the crab is cooked, remove from the steamer, pour over the sauce and serve.

◀

An excavation site at Ban Chiang preserved at the local museum to allow visitors to experience the discovery of the world's oldest culture.

▶

Top left: Pork on Lemon Grass Sticks (*Ka Takrai*), with hot and sweet sauce. Front: Hot and Sour Salad with Crab and Lemon Grass (*Plaa Poo*); Mekong Whisky.

PORK ON LEMON GRASS STICKS (H)

KA TAKRAI

10 oz/300 g minced/ground pork
1 tbsp finely chopped garlic
1 tsp finely chopped coriander root
½ tsp ground white pepper
½ tsp sugar
½ tsp salt
6 x 4 inch/10 cm lengths of lemon grass stalk
vegetable oil for deep frying
The sauce:
6 tbsp rice vinegar
4 tbsp sugar
½ tsp salt
1 garlic clove, finely chopped
4 small fresh red or green chilies, finely chopped
1 tbsp ground roasted peanuts

First make the sauce. In a small saucepan, heat the vinegar, add the sugar and stir until dissolved. Simmer until a syrup forms. Leave to cool, then pour into a bowl and add the remaining ingredients. Stir and set aside.

Place the pork, garlic, coriander root, pepper, sugar and salt in a bowl and mix well. Mould into 6 balls. Stick a length of lemon grass stalk halfway (about 2 inches/5 cm) into each ball and press the meat mixture firmly on to the lemon grass until you have something resembling a small chicken leg.

Heat a pan of oil for deep frying to 400°F/200°C. Deep fry the pork sticks until they are golden brown. Drain and serve with the sauce.

STEAMED FISH WITH LEMON GRASS (T)

PLA NUNG TAKRAI

1 tbsp finely chopped tender lemon grass
1 tsp finely chopped fresh ginger
4 small fresh red or green chilies, finely chopped
1 whole fish, weighing about 1½ lb/720 g (trout, bream, carp, mullet or salmon would do), cleaned
4 dried Chinese mushrooms, soaked, drained and roughly cut across
2 tbsp light soy sauce
½ tsp sugar
1 tbsp lemon juice
sprinkling of salt

Place half the lemon grass, ginger and chilies inside the fish. Set the fish on a heatproof plate with a slightly raised edge, which will fit into a steamer. Cover the fish with the remaining lemon grass, ginger and chilies. Lay the Chinese mushrooms on top. Pour over the soy sauce, sprinkle with the sugar, pour the lemon juice over and sprinkle with the salt.

Bring water to the boil in the bottom part of a steamer. Place the plate in the upper part, cover and steam for 15–20 minutes, depending on the variety of fish. When cooked through, remove and serve.

MONK'S OLIVES (H)
MIANG PRAH

This is a classic Issan titbit. I call it Monk's Olives because villagers like to prepare it for the monks at the local temple. It is not considered to be food – more a medicine – so it can be 'taken' in the afternoon even though the monks will have had their final meal of the day at noon. The intense bittersweet taste of this mixture is extraordinarily refreshing in a very hot climate.

Although I refer to olives here, the Thai fruit *makok* is somewhere between a fresh olive and a small bitter plum. The first European visitors to Siam used to harbour their boats at a place that was known to the local people as Bangkok – 'the place of the wild plums or olives' – and which is, of course, the present capital of modern Thailand. I have assumed that *makok* will be unobtainable outside Thailand but that fresh olives can be found from time to time.

Betel leaves (see photograph on page 22) come from the betel leaf plant, most commonly found in India, and have no botanical connection with the betel nut, which comes from a palm (*Areca catechu*). The betel leaf is used as an 'envelope' which holds aromatic pastes and spices – in India this is the famous *paan* which is served after a meal. Betel leaves are occasionally obtainable from specialist Indian stores. You can substitute crisp lettuce heart leaves.

2 tbsp finely chopped tender lemon grass
2 tsp finely chopped galangal
6 oz/180 g fresh green olives (*not* pickled), stoned/pitted and finely chopped
½ tsp salt
1 tbsp sugar
½ tsp chili powder
10 betel leaves

In a mortar, pound the lemon grass, add the galangal and pound well, then add the olives. Continue pounding to make a rough paste – not too smooth. Add the salt, sugar and chili powder and mix well.

Turn on to a serving dish and serve with the betel or lettuce leaves. Use a leaf to make an envelope around a teaspoon of paste. Slowly chew this to release the pungent flavours.

FRIED CHICKEN BREAST MARINATED IN LEMON GRASS AND CHILI (F)
GAI TAKRAI

10 oz/300 g boneless chicken breast, with or without skin
1 tbsp finely chopped tender lemon grass
4 small fresh red or green chilies, finely chopped
2 tbsp fish sauce
1 tbsp light soy sauce
1 tsp sugar
2 tbsp vegetable oil
To garnish:
cucumber slices
tomato wedges

Place all the ingredients except the oil in a bowl and stir well, ensuring that the pieces of chicken breast are evenly covered. Leave to marinate for 1 hour.

Heat the oil in a wok or frying pan, and lightly fry the marinated chicken pieces until golden brown all over and cooked through. Drain and place on a serving dish. Slice into ½ inch/1.25 cm pieces. Pour the oil from the pan over the chicken and decorate the plate with cucumber and tomato.

TAMARIND
MAKHAM

Tamarind is an expensive delicacy in Asia. It is not yet common in the West, though the brittle brown, slightly furry pods that protect the fruit, and which look like outsize butter beans, do appear in Indian, Chinese and Thai shops from time to time. An Indian supplier is probably the best source as the tamarind tree grows all over the subcontinent, from where it spread to the East. Its name reflects this origin: *tamr* means dry date and *Hind* is the River Indus.

If you find the dryish pods and break them open you will see that inside there is a dark sticky pulp surrounding up to ten large seeds. The pulp is scraped out and the seeds removed before use. It is more likely, however, that you will simply find paper-wrapped blocks of the compressed pulp, with the seeds already removed (*makham biak*). The pulp can be mixed with sugar to make a delicious sweet, or diluted with hot water to make a refreshing infusion, which is believed to be good for dysentery and a treatment for worms. It is also thought to reduce blood pressure.

In Thai cooking, we most commonly dilute a little of the pulp with water to make tamarind water. This adds a lemony, zesty flavour to a dish. The taste is suprisingly familiar as tamarind is one of the principal ingredients of Worcestershire sauce.

Although rare, you may occasionally come across the young fresh fruit (*makham orn*) in specialist shops and perhaps even the tamarind leaves. When young, the tamarind fruit resembles a large browny-green mangetout/snow pea. The leaves have a lemony-sour taste and can be eaten raw in salads; if cooked, they must only be 'tossed' in at the last moment before serving, lest the taste become too bitter.

Young tamarind can be treated like any fresh vegetable. Keep it in the refrigerator – a week is probably the maximum, provided the fruit was recently imported when you bought it. Throw it out if it is dry.

By contrast, the more familiar sticky pulp, whether you scrape it out of the pods yourself or buy it in ready-compressed blocks, will keep almost indefinitely in a sealed jar, without refrigeration.

Some village people in Thailand grill the seeds, remove the black outer skin, and eat the bitter white 'nut' within. This is very much an acquired taste!

If you cannot get tamarind pulp, either fresh or in blocks, to make tamarind water, you can substitute twice the amount of lemon juice.

◄
A temple festival at Pra That Phanom in north-east Thailand – believers earn merit by coating a statue of the Buddha with little sheets of fine gold leaf.

►
Tamarind (*Makham*) Top: Tamarind pulp (*Makham Biak*). Centre: Tamarind pods and seeds. Bottom left: Young tamarind (*Makham Orn*).

CHICKEN SOUP WITH YOUNG TAMARIND LEAVES (S)
TOM GAI BAI MAKHAAM

16 fl oz/500 ml/2 cups chicken stock

6 oz/180 g boneless chicken, roughly chopped

1 stalk of lemon grass, chopped into 5 or 6 pieces and pounded to crush slightly

5 kaffir lime leaves, roughly chopped

4 small fresh red or green chilies, pounded to crush slightly

2 tbsp fish sauce

1 tbsp lime juice

1 tsp sugar

2 oz/60 g young tamarind leaves

In a large saucepan, heat the stock, add the chicken and bring to the boil. Add the lemon grass, kaffir lime leaves, chilies, fish sauce, lime juice and sugar, stirring well. Simmer until the chicken is cooked through.

Quickly stir in the tamarind leaves, pour into a bowl and serve.

SPARE RIB AND TAMARIND SOUP (S)
TOM SOM

1 tsp black peppercorns

1 tsp finely chopped coriander root

1 garlic clove, peeled

2 small shallots, peeled

½ tsp dried shrimp paste

1 tbsp vegetable oil

16 fl oz/500 ml/2 cups chicken stock

1 lb/480 g small pork spare ribs chopped into 1 inch/2.5 cm pieces

1 inch/2.5 cm piece of fresh ginger, peeled and finely slivered into matchsticks

2 tbsp tamarind water (page 142)

1 tbsp sugar

2 tbsp fish sauce

2 spring onions/scallions, chopped into 1 inch/2.5 cm lengths

In a mortar, pound together the peppercorns, coriander root, garlic and shallots. When well pounded, add the shrimp paste and pound together to a paste.

In a large saucepan, heat the oil and fry the paste for 5 seconds, stirring well. Add the stock and bring to the boil, stirring well. Add the spare ribs and bring back to the boil. Add all the remaining ingredients. Return to the boil again and simmer for 1 minute. Turn into a bowl and serve.

SOUR PRAWN/SHRIMP CURRY (C)
GAENG SOM

1¾ pints/1 litre/4 cups chicken stock

1 lb/480 g small raw prawns/shrimp, peeled and de-veined

4 tbsp tamarind water (page 142)

3 tbsp fish sauce

2 tbsp sugar

2 oz/60 g/⅔ cup Chinese leaf/Napa cabbage, roughly chopped

2 oz/60 g/¼ cup bamboo shoots, roughly chopped

2 oz/60 g/½ cup white radish (mooli/daikon) roughly chopped

2 oz/60 g/½ cup long beans, chopped into 1 inch/2.5 cm lengths

The curry paste:

1 oz/30 g dry chilies, roughly chopped

2 oz/60 g shallots, peeled

2 tsp dried shrimp paste

½ tsp salt

First make the curry paste. In a mortar, pound the chilies well, add the shallots and continue pounding. Add the shrimp paste and salt and pound together to a paste. Set aside.

Put half the prawns into the mortar and pound them to a paste.

In a large saucepan, heat the stock, add the curry paste and stir well. Add the pounded prawns and stir. Add the tamarind water, fish sauce and sugar and stir well. Add the remaining whole prawns. Then, stirring constantly, add the vegetables in turn.

Return to the boil and simmer until the vegetables are just cooked *al dente*. Turn into a bowl and serve.

YOUNG TAMARIND SPICY DIP (D)
NAM PRIK MAKHAM ORN

4 oz/120 g fresh young tamarind fruit

1 tbsp chopped garlic

5 small fresh red or green chilies

1 tbsp dried shrimp paste

2 tbsp vegetable oil

4 oz/120 g minced/ground pork

1 tbsp fish sauce

2 tbsp sugar

In a mortar, pound the tamarind until they are well broken up. Add the garlic and chilies and pound together well. Add the shrimp paste and pound together to a paste. Set aside.

In a wok or frying pan, heat the oil and fry the pork until it is white and crumbly. Stir in the paste and mix well. Stirring constantly, add the fish sauce and then the sugar. Stir well.

Turn into a bowl and serve as a dip with pieces of raw, crunchy vegetables such as small green or round aubergines/eggplants (page 61), long beans, cucumber and carrots.

142

TAMARIND WATER
NAM SOM MAKHAM

The commonest form of tamarind found in the West is blocks of the dark sticky pulp. In Thai cuisine this is most often made into tamarind water and is used in many recipes. Tamarind pulp can be kept in a jar, without refrigeration. Tamarind water can be kept in a jar, in the refrigerator, for up to a week.

1 tsp tamarind pulp
¼ pint/150 ml/⅔ cup hot water

Mix the pulp and hot water together in a bowl. Leave to soak for 24 hours. Squeeze the softened pulp to get all the juices into the liquid, then discard the pulp.

▲
Oyster mushrooms, *nang rom*, occasionally available in oriental stores but similar to the French *pleurotte* mushroom.

▶
Three Flavoured Fish (*Pla Sam Rut*).

THREE FLAVOURED FISH (F)
PLA SAM RUT

2 tbsp finely chopped garlic

2 large fresh red chilies, finely chopped

1 medium-size, firm-fleshed fish, suitable for deep frying (bream or sea bass would do), cleaned

vegetable oil for deep frying + 2 tbsp

2 tbsp palm sugar

3 tbsp fish sauce

2 tbsp tamarind water (page 142)

In a mortar, pound the garlic and chilies together. Set aside.

Rinse the fish and pat dry. Heat a pan of oil for deep frying to 400°F/200°C. Deep fry the fish until golden and crispy. Drain and place on a serving dish. Keep hot.

Heat the 2 tablespoons of oil in a wok or frying pan, and stir in the pounded garlic and chilies. Add the palm sugar and stir, then stir in the fish sauce and tamarind water. Pour over the deep-fried fish and serve.

CHICKEN WITH TAMARIND (H)
SANG WA

The Thai name for this dish – *Sang Wa* – is an old way of saying 'pretend', and I suspect that this is because the ingredients here are substitutes for other, more difficult ones. The original dish was probably a southern speciality made with fish stomach, but as its popularity spread inland, so those away from the sea decided to make a pretend version with chicken.

2 large chicken breasts, total weight about 8 oz/240 g

3 tbsp tamarind water (page 142)

2 tbsp fish sauce

1 tbsp sugar

1 tbsp lime juice

2 inch/5 cm piece of young lemon grass, finely sliced into rings

2 tbsp fresh ginger slivered into very fine matchsticks

6 small shallots, finely chopped into ovals

3 kaffir lime leaves, rolled into a cigarette shape and finely sliced across

1 large fresh red chili/*prik chee faa*, finely sliced into ovals

crisp lettuce leaves, to serve

fresh coriander leaves/cilantro, to garnish

Preheat the grill/broiler.

Grill/broil the chicken breasts until golden brown and cooked through. With your fingers, tear the meat into small shreds and set aside.

In a small saucepan, heat the tamarind water, fish sauce and sugar, stirring until the sugar dissolves. Remove from the heat and add the lemon juice. Stir in the shredded chicken, mixing well. Add the lemon grass, ginger, shallots and kaffir lime leaf and stir well. Add the chili and stir.

Arrange the lettuce leaves around a platter and place the chicken mixture in the centre. Garnish with coriander leaves and serve.

FRIED MOONG BEAN PASTE WITH TAMARIND SAUCE (VH)
TUA TONG

Moong beans (mung or green gram) are small dried yellow beans available from oriental stores. The soaking time varies depending on the recipe.

4 oz/120 ml dried moong beans
1 tbsp rice flour
½ tsp ground white pepper
1 tsp ground cumin
½ tsp salt
1 tsp sugar
vegetable oil for deep frying
The tamarind sauce/nam jim makaam:
3 large fresh red chilies/*prik chee faa*, roughly chopped
1 large garlic clove, roughly chopped
3 large shallots, roughly chopped
3 tbsp tamarind water (page 142)
1 tbsp sugar
½ tsp salt

Soak the moong beans in water for 30 minutes.

Meanwhile, make the sauce. In a mortar, pound together the chilies, garlic and shallots. When well pounded, stir in the tamarind water, sugar and salt and mix well together. Turn into a small bowl.

Drain the beans, then put in a mortar and pound until well broken and soft. Transfer to a bowl and mix in all the other ingredients, except the oil, to form a thick paste. Roll pieces of the paste into small balls about 1 inch/2.5 cm diameter.

Heat the oil and deep fry the balls until golden brown. Drain on paper towels and serve with the sauce.

FISH PICKLE WITH COCONUT AND TAMARIND (D)
LON PLA RAA

This is a north-eastern stand-by – once the great jar of fish-pickle has been made, it is easy to dip into it at any time to make a quick relish like this to go with a large plate of rice.

8 fl oz/240 ml/1 cup fish pickle/*pla raa*
16 fl oz/480 ml/2 cups coconut cream (page 178)
2 tbsp tamarind water (page 142)
1 tsp sugar
20 small shallots, sliced into ovals
5 large fresh red chilies/*prik chee faa*, roughly chopped into 5 pieces each
crudités: crisp lettuce, cucumber, celery, radishes, etc., to serve.

Remove any bones from the fish and chop into very small flakes. In a small saucepan, heat the coconut cream, add the fish pickle and stir well. Stir in the remaining ingredients and gently bring to the boil, stirring well. Simmer to reduce the liquid. When a thick sauce has formed, turn into a bowl and serve as a dip with crudités. This pickle does not have to be served hot.

4

HEADING
SOUTH

◆

SOUTHERN
THAILAND
AND THE
ISLANDS

148 It is just before sunset and a noise like gunfire echoes across the entrance to the harbour of the southern city of Songkhla. There are still pirates loose in the Gulf of Thailand, but this is not the sound of a sea-battle. It is only the local fishermen setting off noisy fire-crackers as they leave for the fishing grounds, hoping that the explosions will summon Mae Ya Nang, the Goddess of Water, to accompany them on their journey. In the hope that she will ride along with them, they decorate the prows of their boats with flowers and coloured scarves, and no woman is ever allowed to sit there, lest the Goddess be jealous. Like fisherfolk everywhere, these sailors are deeply superstitious – they will only boil or quickly fry fish on board as grilling might burn the flesh and turn away the shoals of fish through which they pass. Even the way they prepare the fish has its rules – many believe that they should never turn a fish as they fillet it, in case this causes the boat to capsize.

For all this, these are marvellous fishermen and it is well worth going to the market on the docks of Songkhla when the boats return, to watch the muscled wiry men in their striped breach-clouts, the lucky tattoos prominent on the upper arms, unloading sea bass, shark, herring, pomfret, prawns/shrimp, lobster, crab, tuna, mackerel, squid, eel, oysters – all the bounty of Mae Ya Nang. This fish market is one of the largest in South East Asia. An acute sense of smell is of no benefit if you plan to wander among the giant baskets of wriggling glistening fish, past the jovial women who squat at their chopping boards, trimming, gutting and filleting, as the catch is showered with crushed ice for the buyers in white shirts and trousers who parade about, scribbling in notebooks and haggling over the price. The smell is indescribable: the pong of ages; a paradise on earth for stray animals; cat heaven. Best not to breathe too deeply and to concentrate instead on the pleasures to come: a whole pomfret simmered in tamarind juice; oysters tossed in a spicy omelette; a 'beachcomber's hotplate' of stewed fish with prawns and sweetcorn; kingfish in a piquant mango salad; crab fried with curry.

These are quite complex dishes, but most Thai seafood cooking is essentially simple – you grill a fish and serve it with a piquant sauce. It was this easy simplicity that first opened up the South to visitors some twenty years ago, when hippies began to island-hop around the coast of Thailand, once word got out that they could live incredibly cheaply, sleeping on beaches and eating freshly caught fish from the crystal waters. As more and more outsiders came, once isolated islands such as Koh Samui in the Western Gulf, and Phi Phi Island and Phuket in the Adaman Sea, began to offer a few beachside huts and

◄◄
The giant statue of the Buddha at Ban Bo Phut watches over the island of Koh Samui in the southern Gulf of Thailand.

the occasional spot under the palms where fish were grilled and drinks served and perhaps a little music played. Of course, it was then just a short step to the first beach bungalows, then the tower block hotels, then the resort complexes, until things came round full circle and Club Méditerranée arrived to offer its guests a simulacrum of a holiday hut on a beach! Happily, the main tourist activities are concentrated in clusters with quite a bit of less-frequented space still left in between.

Those first young travellers were able to get into the region so easily thanks to the charming narrow-gauge railway that meanders right down the isthmus before crossing into Malaysia and travelling on, all the way to Singapore. It is still one of the classic experiences of Asian travel to leave Bangkok's imposing Hua Lampong Station, with its beamed booking halls and Italianate tiled floors, and to pass out through the endless city sprawl, with ramshackle dwellings huddled right up to the tracks, offering glimpses of the ant-hill existence of Bangkok's poor. Some even appear to live in the spaces beneath the bridges and viaducts across which the train slowly makes its way. Out, at last, over the fields and farmlands of the Western Gulf. *En route*, there are frequent stops at quaint fretwork stations that resemble gingerbread houses in a Victorian print. Meals are served at your table and the large comfortable seats are transformed into beds as night falls. The Eastern Oriental Express, similar in luxury to the London-Venice pullman, now makes this journey with every imaginable amenity to pamper the high-paying traveller. For me, however, the old train is thrilling enough, with plenty of stops if one wants to make a side trip into the surrounding countryside or out to the nearby islands.

The South really begins at the city of Petchaburi, 165 kilometres south-west of Bangkok and a major centre for food lovers. Thais visit the city primarily because it is the 'sweet-tooth' capital of the country. This is said to be due to its many varieties of palm, each producing a subtly different flavoured palm sugar. Palm sugar is the basic ingredient for *kanom*, the solid desserts that are offered for sale at large sweetmeat markets set out in roadside pavilions, just outside the town. Travellers can load up with trays of baked custard or packets of brightly coloured coconut sweets, great gifts for friends and family back home.

The rich caramel taste of palm sugar is not just used for confectionery. Thais also like the flavour it adds to the sweet and hot fish dish, *Nam Plow Wan*. Thai cooking is quite liberal about mixing sweet and savoury flavours – one of the best loved custards, *Kanom*

Maw Gaeng, is sometimes served with a sprinkling of fried shallots! Fruits are much used, and the South abounds with suitable ingredients: intensely sweet pineapples and twenty-eight varieties of banana, as well as those luscious tropical fruits: papaya, pomelo, mango and lychee. Many southern dishes also rely on one or more of the three ginger flavours – ginger itself, galangal and turmeric. These add a sweet dimension to savoury dishes such as *Moo Pad King Grob*, where the pork is served with crispy fried ginger.

But I don't want to leave the impression that we only visit Petchaburi for the food. The town is also famous for its temple murals. Its equable climate has long made it a popular holiday centre, especially for the royal family. This has resulted in a number of spectacular architectural beauty spots. The most famous of these is King Mongkut's brilliant white hilltop palace, which looks down on the town and can now be visited by a convenient funicular railway.

I am especially fond of a less accessible royal building, largely because it took me so many attempts to get inside. *Pa Ra Wang Bahn Bhun*, a royal hunting lodge, stands on the southern outskirts of Petchaburi and is quite unique among royal homes in Thailand. King Chulalangkorn the Great wanted a holiday guest house for foreign princes, who he knew would like to hunt the game that was abundant in the wooded hillsides further to the south. The king had visited the German Kaiser at the end of the last century and had much admired one of his Bavarian residences; so in 1910, a German master-builder was brought to Thailand to create a slightly smaller replica. Unfortunately, the king died almost as soon as work began. His successor, King Rama VI, the same king who tried to create a masterplan for Bangkok, finished the work as a pious filial duty, but he never used the completed building. Over the years, it simply stood there, shuttered but taken care of by the local Royal Guard.

On various visits to the town, I attempted to persuade the sentries to let me see inside the lodges, but was only ever permitted to walk around the grounds since no one seemed to have a key that could let

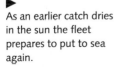

◀
Painting the prow of a fishing vessel near Songhkla.

▶
As an earlier catch dries in the sun the fleet prepares to put to sea again.

me in. I finally succeeded when I happened to turn up on a day when a group of army cadets was being taken in to pay homage to the statues of the two kings that stand in the lodge's grand entrance. I followed and, as I had always expected, the interior turned out to be quite amazing, a perfectly preserved art nouveau palace, with tall columns decorated with multicoloured tiles, and elaborate lamps in the belle époque manner. There is some talk that the lodge may eventually be opened to the public, but until then, if you want to visit it, try asking the sergeant on duty at the local barracks if there is any chance of getting in. You never know, you might be lucky. My own visit ended with the bizarre experience of stepping through dozens of pairs of highly polished army boots, neatly lined up at the front door by the cadets who, in best Thai fashion, had entered the residence bare-foot.

Leaving Petchaburi you can continue your train journey south, getting off at Surat Thani for a short detour to Don Sak to catch the ferry to the island of Koh Samui. You may be disappointed at first because the little town there seems to be entirely given over to tour operators and car hire firms. Even when you drive around the coast road, the edge of the island seems to be one long bungalow resort. But this is deceptive, for the interior is still a vast forest of coconut palms.

Before the hippies arrived and transformed the island into a paradise for snorklers and wind-surfers, coconut growing was the basis of the local economy, a position it still holds today – over two million coconuts are said to be despatched to Bangkok every month, testimony to the important role coconut milk plays in Thai cooking. I had a choice example of this during my last stay, one that also proved that you cannot simply rule out modern tourist resorts, many of which try hard to keep up with the Thai tradition of good food. I had chosen one – 'World Bungalow' – entirely at random, only to find that its young chef, Khun Sak Da, was a highly original technician who had some inventive ways with the local produce. His white snapper, deep fried with pineapple, was so good I now serve it in my restaurant under the title *Pla Samui*, or Samui Fish. The local coconut came in the form of *Tod Man Poo*, little crab and coconut cakes served with a salty-sweet, preserved-plum sauce.

If you hire a vehicle of some sort you can always get away from the crowds for another view of the island. At one point I left the main road that traverses the interior, to follow a sign pointing to a temple somewhere lost among the trees. Leaving the car, I walked along a narrow track until I came to a shady compound that seemed to be completely deserted. There were pretty little lodges for monks, with the same gingerbread decoration as the railway stations, and a large old prayer hall. This I managed to open and found it to be filled with rows of forgotten Buddhas, all carved out of grey pumice from the sea, silent watchers, lit only by the slatted light filtering in from under the eaves.

Outside again, I thought I heard a faint noise and following it, I came to a pavilion where all the monks were sitting cross-legged, watching a flickering television. They all had that slightly puzzled look that only the truly innocent have – the Gulf War had just begun and these isolated holy men were studying the images from CNN News of Scud missiles flashing across the Baghdad skyline. Occasionally, one of the monks would make a comment and the others would nod sagely, no doubt trying to work out as best they could what it all meant.

No one would pretend that islands like Koh Samui are weighed down with culture. At Ban Bo Phut beach, a massive 40 ft/12 m high Buddha sits atop a spit of land jutting into the sea, guarding the waters, a sight doubly impressive at sunset when the huge figure is silhouetted against the darkening sky. But that aside, you go for the sun, the sea and the food, and why not? If you want more, all you have to do is continue south on the train to Nakhorn Si Thammarat, the last major city before Songhkla, and one of Thailand's principle artistic centres.

For sheer size it is hard to better the 236 ft/72 m high golden *chedi* or spire of Wat Mahathat, nor the amazing collection of precious artifacts in its dusty museum. But the city has more than ancient art: it is famous for its living crafts too. The art of nielloware, in which gold plated dishes and bowls are incised with intricate patterns, and then filled in with black lead to leave a bold decorative effect, was revived in the city some sixty years ago.

I was even more fascinated to see one of the rare examples of Thai classical puppetry, which still survives in Nakhorn. A short walk from Wat Mahathat I found the modest home and workshop of puppet-master Khun Suchart Subsin. A famous practitioner, he makes and sells the traditional dried cow-hide figures of princes and demons with hands and mouths, operated by thin bamboo sticks, that spring to life at the touch of an expert. Khun Suchart gives performances from behind a screen in the little theatre he has built in his garden. When I was there, I joined an audience of mostly young people watching spellbound as the well-known mythological characters were put through their paces. Khun Suchart and his assistant took all the parts and performed all the voices in a dizzying array of quick changes. I soon realized, however, that while the characters were ancient, the play was not the usual tale from the epic Ramakien, the poetic drama of the struggle between gods, men and demons that is the basis of much of Thailand's classical culture. The puppet-master had decided to give his young audience a little play which warned them of the dangers of AIDS and the need to practise safe sex – a useful adaptation of an ancient art form to an urgent contemporary problem.

From Nakhorn Si Thamarat, the railway will take you as far as the city of Hat Yai, from where you must travel by road the 25 kilometres to Songhkla. The two places could not be more different. Hat Yai is another booming modern metropolis, though for the food-lover it does have the odd distinction of probably being the canned food capital of Asia. Because of its proximity to the border, Malaysians come to buy Thai produce, while Thais come to buy Malaysian goods, all of which makes Hat Yai's markets a cosmopolitan treasure trove. There is much Malay Muslim influence in the deep south of Thailand. The mosque in Pattani, near the frontier, could have been transported intact from Arabia, and one of our richest dishes, Mussaman curry, is pungent with the sorts of spices more often associated with Indian and Arabic cooking.

Songhkla, by contrast, combines Muslim with Chinese influences. The sleepy coastal town itself has a number of surviving Chinese town houses with elegantly upswept roofs and slightly inward sloping walls. The most imposing is the old Governor's Palace, built in 1878, and now a national museum. There are shady courtyards with upper verandas that lead into the main reception rooms, whose polished teak floors, red laquer furniture and stiffly formal photographs of bemedalled officials, evoke an age when the governors were all-powerful, and the king in faraway Bangkok was too remote to do more than ask for his revenues to be paid.

Following the coast road out of town you come to a small Muslim fishing village where the *kolae* boats are drawn up on the beach, allowing visitors to admire the intricacy of the coloured designs painted on their prows. Every house in the village seems to have its drying frame where squid, shrimps and small fish are left out in the sun to dry and brown, then to be grilled and served with a hot sweet sauce. If you return to the town and go around to the Samila Beach which faces inland, you will find over twenty seafood restaurants lining the coast road, all serving simple grills with piquant sauces. For more elaborate dishes, you must travel out to the little island of Koh Yor in the Songhkla 'Lake', a vast inland sea and a

famous local beauty spot with a number of stilt restaurants perched
at the water's edge. Friends took me to their favourite restaurant, *Ko
Kheng*, where the speciality is black king crabs and oyster omelettes,
but where I, rather perversely, chose to eat *Moo Koh Yor*, hot and sour
grilled pork with green mango, a change from what had become an
unremitting diet of seafood.

Songhkla is still a sleepy, half-forgotten place, not yet firmly on
the tourist trail. That honour belongs to the largest island of all,
Phuket, on the other side of the isthmus on the Andaman Sea. The
strip of land that divides Thailand from Malaysia narrows, and there
is no problem making the journey west from Songhkla in a shared
taxi. You drive through spectacular wooded gorges to Krabi, where
there are plenty of boats to ferry you across to one of Thailand's most
developed holiday resorts.

I first visited Phuket the very day the new International Airport
was opened, when it was still possible to enjoy the sort of secluded
beach-hut holiday that was about to disappear. Today, Phuket caters

▼
It is said that some two
million coconuts are sent
to Bangkok every
month, from the little
island of Koh Samui
alone!

156   for everyone, from the cheap package tourists to those individuals able to pay for the ultimate in exclusive luxury. The last time I went, I had a rare chance to see that other, secretive world of the super-rich, having been invited to stay at the Amanpuri, reputedly the most private resort on the island. Having crossed from Krabi by ferry and unable to find a taxi, I was forced to hire a battered minibus that coughed and spluttered its way around the narrow roads as my driver attempted to find this hidden place – the Amanpuri does not bother with signs as its guests normally travel from the airport in a chauffeur-driven Mercedes. I must be the first person to have arrived in a filthy *song tel*, but at least the receptionist managed to hide her surprise.

I would like to say how indifferent I was to what the Amanpuri had to offer, but that would be a lie. It was stunningly beautiful, a collection of elegant Thai wooden buildings arranged at the top of a cliff, looking out over the sea. Each guest or couple has an individual pavilion with its own Thai *sala*, an open room where you can sit and look out over the waters as you nibble the fruit that is constantly being replenished by unseen servants (I guess they must lurk in the undergrowth). As there are only forty of these rooms, nestled among the coconut palms, you hardly feel crowded. The heart of the resort is a long rectangular swimming pool that seems to run right over the cliff to join the distant sea – a stunning optical illusion, enhanced at night by lights, hidden in the surrounding palms, which turn the surface of the pool into a sheer mirror. To one side are two restaurants, Thai and Italian; on the other is an open pavilion in which sits a Thai gamalin orchestra, its musicians dressed in cloth of gold. When I came down the wooden walkways from my room for my evening drink, I was so struck by the beauty of it all that I hurried back to get my camera, only to discover that the lurking servants had leapt into action – my recently vacated bathroom had been cleaned and arranged, my bedroom tidied and the bedsheets turned down, and yet another massive bowl of fruit was set out in my *sala*.

Wondering how they had managed this extraordinary feat, I returned to the glittering pool and crossed to the restaurant, expecting that here at least I would meet up with reality. Given my belief that the best Thai cooking is usually found in the least prepossessing surroundings, it hardly seemed likely that so elegant a place could offer anything but mediocre food. In fact, I was in for two surprises. First, the Thai cooking was not only good, it was inventive; I was most surprised to discover a brilliant version of the ordinary satay dish that one finds everywhere today. These grilled slivers of meat served with a peanut sauce came originally from Malaysia, though the Thai version, served with a fresh pickle, much enhances the original. At the Amanpuri, the meat was replaced by giant prawns, split, skewered and grilled and served with the peanut sauce and pickle. Even more surprising than this clever invention was the discovery that it had been created not by one of the Thai chefs, but by a young Italian who had been learning about Thai food and had seen a neat way to make something pretty and tasty and well-suited to the seaside.

The limited number of guests, and the clever way in which each of the Thai pavilions is isolated amongst the trees, makes the Amanpuri the nearest one can now get to the sort of beach holiday I used to enjoy before tourism took over. The irony is that what students and hippies used to enjoy for free is now only available to the exceptionally wealthy. I used to dream of having my own stretch of beach, with my own hut under my own palm tree, but I have had to accept that this is now impossible – every inch of beach in Thailand seems to have been bought by someone, and there is nowhere so remote that you might not wake up one morning to the sound of workmen blasting the foundations for yet another holiday resort. I have had to be content with buying an isolated plot of land, a one-time rice paddy, outside Petchaburi, where I have built a simple wooden cabin and drilled for water to make a pond, around which my bananas and mangos are starting to sprout. If I want to go swimming, the beach is only 20 minutes away. If I want seafood, I head for the Tap Tim Tom Restaurant at Bahn Lam, just beyond the town, which is built on a wooden pier over the mudflats where the local people dig for shellfish at low tide. These are served up, steamed with krachai, an unexpectedly vivid combination, with the tangy gingery taste lifting the fishy flavours of the molluscs to new heights. There is usually a pleasant breeze at the Tap Tim Tom, and after the meal one can sit back and watch the boats chugging to and from the fishing grounds, skirting the miniature wooden houses that rise out of the water, that were built as dwellings for the original spirit of the place, to placate him for our intrusion on his territory.

I have a spirit house on my own piece of land, and I always leave an offering of drink and flowers so that the spirit Phra Poum will look kindly upon my presence there. Seated by my quiet pond, I can watch the sun set over the distant hills, only a short drive from the Burmese border. And then, when it grows dark, I can use my generator to light my outside kitchen, where I can cook my evening meal on a charcoal stove – as near to the simple life as one can hope to get in an overcrowded world.

GINGER AND GALANGAL
KING, KHAA

There are several plants that impart a 'gingery' flavour, each with a slightly different intensity or with a subtle addition, such as the lemony-ginger taste of galangal, or the slightly hot-ginger taste of turmeric. All four – ginger, galangal, krachai and turmeric – are very similar and are often referred to as roots although they are in fact rhizomes, or stems that grow underground.

Ginger
Ginger, often called 'root ginger or ginger root', was until recently more often seen as preserved sweet ginger in jars or as ground ginger, which could be rather musty and unpleasant. Fortunately, the knobbly, golden-beige 'fingers' of fresh ginger are now quite common in markets and stores.

The highly skilled art of the Thai fruit and vegetable carver – we ordinary mortals can usually manage a simple chili flower.

An infusion of ginger and water is good for stomach disorders, including morning sickness during pregnancy, it is also taken as a stimulant.

There are several varieties of ginger grown in Thailand, each with its own unique properties. One can also get young fresh ginger that is tender enough to be stir-fried as if it were a vegetable. In Thai cuisine, ginger is often eaten raw as a spicy nibble with dips or sausages. For this purpose, it is essential to select only the youngest, tenderest rhizomes. Older ginger is too fibrous and dry although it is quite acceptable if cooked. Recipes usually recommend that you peel a piece of ginger, then sliver it into thin matchsticks so that it will cook thoroughly and be easily digestible.

If you find any young ginger (it will be more pink in colour) you should rush to buy it. Whether young or old, choose 'roots' that are firm and not shrivelled or marked. Wrapped well, in clingfilm/plastic wrap, ginger can be kept for up to 2 weeks in the refrigerator.

Galangal
This rhizome was immensely popular in late medieval Europe, but has not been much used in western cooking in more recent centuries. It is now returning, thanks to the popularity of oriental cuisines. Like its cousin ginger it is good for stomach problems, especially nausea. While slightly harder than ginger, it is used in exactly the same way – peeled and most often slivered into matchsticks or finely sliced into thin 'rounds' in order to cook thoroughly. It can be kept, well wrapped, in the refrigerator for two weeks.

▶
Ginger (*King*);
Galangal (*Khaa*)

RECIPES

WITH GINGER AND GALANGAL

CHICKEN, COCONUT AND GALANGAL SOUP (S)

GAI TOM KA

16 fl oz/500 ml/2 cups chicken stock

2 kaffir lime leaves

1 inch/2.5 cm piece of galangal, peeled and split lengthways into several pieces

2 tbsp fish sauce

3 tbsp lemon juice

4 oz/120 g boneless, skinless chicken breast, finely sliced

4 fl oz/120 ml/ ½ cup coconut milk (page 178)

2 small fresh red chilies, slightly crushed with the flat of a large knife

fresh coriander leaves/cilantro, to garnish

In a saucepan, heat the stock and add the lime leaves, galangal, fish sauce and lemon juice. Stirring well, bring to the boil. Add the chicken and the coconut milk. Continue to cook over a high heat, stirring constantly, until the meat is cooked through (about 2 minutes). Add the crushed chilies for the last few seconds.

Pour into small bowls, garnish with coriander leaves and serve.

CHICKEN AND GINGER SALAD (H)

MIANG GAI

8 oz/240 g minced/ground chicken

2 tbsp fish sauce

2 tbsp lemon juice

1 tsp sugar

4 small fresh red or green chilies, finely chopped

1 inch/2.5 cm piece of fresh ginger, peeled and cut into fine matchsticks

4 oz/120 g carrots, cut into fine matchsticks

4 oz/120 g/1 cup fresh beansprouts

2 oz/60 g/6 tbsp roasted peanuts

prawn/shrimp crackers, to serve

If necessary, fry the prawn crackers according to the instructions on the packet. Set aside.

Put the chicken into a wok or frying pan and stir in the fish sauce, lemon juice, sugar and chilies. Cook, stirring well so that the meat doesn't form lumps. Keep stirring until the meat is cooked through, then remove the pan from the heat and stir in the ginger, carrots, beansprouts and peanuts.

Turn on to a dish and serve with prawn crackers.

FRIED FISH WITH GINGER AND PINEAPPLE (F)

PLA SAMUI

selection of shredded white cabbage, chopped tomato, cucumber slices and pineapple segments

vegetable oil for deep frying

1 medium-size trout or similar firm-fleshed fish, cleaned

The sauce:

2 tbsp fish sauce

2 tbsp lime juice

1 tbsp palm sugar

2 oz/60 g fresh ginger, peeled and cut into fine matchsticks

3 shallots, finely chopped

2 spring onions/scallions, finely chopped

4 small fresh red or green chilies, finely chopped

Arrange the vegetables and pineapple on a large serving platter. Set aside.

Prepare the sauce before frying the fish. In a bowl, stir together the fish sauce, lime juice and palm sugar, stirring until the sugar has dissolved. Stirring constantly, add the other ingredients in turn. Mix thoroughly.

Heat a pan of oil for deep frying to 400°F/200°C. Deep fry the fish until it is golden and cooked through, turning once or twice. Lift out of the oil and drain on paper towels, then place on top of the vegetables. Pour over the prepared sauce.

PORK FRIED WITH CRISPY GINGER (F)
MOO PAD KING GROB

8 oz/240 g boneless pork, roughly chopped
1 tbsp sesame oil
1 tsp cornflour/cornstarch
½ tsp salt
2 tbsp vegetable oil
2 tbsp finely chopped fresh ginger
1 tbsp fish sauce
1 tbsp light soy sauce
1 tsp sugar
½ tsp ground white pepper
fresh coriander leaves/cilantro, to garnish

Put the pork, sesame oil, cornflour and salt into a bowl and stir well to ensure that the meat is evenly coated. Leave to marinate for 30 minutes.

In a wok or frying pan, heat the vegetable oil and fry the ginger until crispy. Add the marinated pork and stir-fry until the meat is white. Add all the remaining ingredients and stir well.

Turn on to a serving dish and garnish with coriander leaves.

SQUID STUFFED WITH PORK AND GALANGAL (T)
PLA MUK SONGKLA

6 baby squid, cleaned, weighing about 7 oz/210 g
6 oz/180 g minced/ground pork
2 tsp finely chopped galangal
1 medium-size onion, finely chopped
1 tbsp fish sauce
1 tbsp oyster sauce
1 tsp sugar
½ tsp ground white pepper
1 tbsp sesame oil

Lightly score the outside of each of the squid 'sacks' with diagonal cross cuts to make a diamond pattern.

In a bowl, mix together all the remaining ingredients except the sesame oil, stirring well. Divide into 6 equal portions and use to stuff the squid sacks. Place the stuffed squid on a heatproof plate with a raised edge. Sprinkle with the sesame oil.

Bring water to the boil in the bottom part of a steamer. Place the plate in the top part of the steamer, cover and steam for 10–15 minutes or until tender, depending on the size and thickness of the squid. Remove from the steamer and serve.

KRACHAI AND TURMERIC
KRACHAI, KHAMIN

Krachai is sometimes called 'lesser ginger', but this rhizome has a subtly different, slightly lemony flavour that makes it quite different from common ginger. It is, however, used and kept in exactly the same ways.

Turmeric has a warm spicy taste and provides a rich orange-yellow colour that will brighten up any dish in which it appears. It is the cause of the somewhat lurid yellow colour of the Anglo-Indian piccalilli, and in parts of Asia it is used as a dye and a cosmetic.

Until recently, the turmeric sold in Europe and North America had been boiled, peeled and sun-dried before exportation, and it was more usual to buy ready-ground turmeric powder to be used as a spice for curries.

Today you can sometimes find the uncooked rhizomes in specialist shops. These should be treated in the same way as ginger, galangal or krachai.

If you are using turmeric powder as a spice, buy only a little at a time, as it soon becomes musty and loses its vivid flavour and aroma.

◀
Cat heaven – the fish market.

▶
Krachai (*Krachai*), left, and turmeric (*Khamin*), right.

RECIPES

STEAMED MUSSELS WITH KRACHAI (H)
HOY OP KRACHAI

1 lb/480 g mussels

2 oz/60 g krachai, peeled and cut into fine matchsticks

20 fresh holy basil leaves

The sauce:

2 garlic cloves, finely chopped

2 tbsp lemon juice

2 tbsp fish sauce

1 tbsp light soy sauce

1 tsp sugar

4 small fresh red or green chilies, finely chopped

1 tbsp ground roasted peanuts

First make the sauce. Place all the ingredients in a mixing bowl and mix well. Pour into a small serving dish and set aside.

Scrub the mussels thoroughly under cold running water, scraping off any barnacles, or 'beards'. Put the mussels in a heavy-based pan on a high heat. Thrown in the krachai and basil leaves and stir, then cover the pan. Leave a moment, then lift and shake the pan to toss the mussels and spread the ingredients. Repeat this process over a period of 5–8 minutes or until the shells have opened. Discard any mussels that have not opened.

Ladle on to a serving dish and serve with the sauce. You can eat the krachai, take just a little bit with each mussel.

FRIED CURRIED FISH WITH KRACHAI (F)
PAD PET PLA DUK

In Thailand this recipe is always used for river fish, the staple protein of many Thai villagers. Here it's catfish, but river trout or similar river fish would be a good substitute. Poor people survive through a large intake of rice which needs to be helped down with something very savoury. Quite small amounts of fish with chili and spices will go a long way. Thais like to cook fish with krachai as it reduces the odour while the fish is cooking.

1 whole catfish, weighing about 10 oz/300 g

vegetable oil for frying + 1 tbsp

1 tbsp red curry paste (page 89)

4 tbsp coconut cream (page 178)

2 tbsp krachai (approx 3 small rhizomes), slivered into fine matchsticks

2 tbsp fish sauce

1 tbsp sugar

3 kaffir lime leaves, rolled into a cigarette shape and finely slivered across

2 large fresh red chilies/*prik chee faa*, sliced into ovals

Clean the fish and cut across into 1 inch/2.5 cm slices. Heat a pan of oil for deep frying to 400°F/200°C. Deep fry the fish slices until hard but not yet crispy. Drain and set aside.

In a wok or frying pan, heat 1 tablespoon of oil, add the red curry paste and stir well until it begins to blend with the oil (2–3 seconds). Add half the coconut cream and blend, then add the deep-fried fish and stir until well coated with the mixture. Add the remaining coconut cream and stir well. Stirring between each addition, add all the remaining ingredients in turn. After a final stir, turn on to a dish and serve.

CURRIED FISH PATTIES (C)
GAENG SAP NOK

8 oz/240 g white fish fillet (cod, haddock or similar), flaked

1 tbsp red curry paste (page 89)

8 fl oz/240 ml/1 cup coconut cream (page 178)

1 oz/30 g krachai, peeled and cut into fine matchsticks

4 oz/120 g/1 cup long beans, cut into 1 inch/2.5 cm pieces

2 tbsp fish sauce

8 fl oz/240 ml/1 cup chicken stock

1 tbsp light soy sauce

1 tsp sugar

3 kaffir lime leaves, roughly chopped

10 fresh sweet basil leaves

In a mortar, pound the flaked fish until smooth. Using your hands, squeeze and knead it to a paste. Set aside.

In a large saucepan, heat the curry paste with the coconut cream, stirring well. Make small patties about 1 inch/2.5 cm in diameter out of the fish paste and put them into the simmering liquid. Add all the other ingredients and stir gently. Simmer, stirring frequently, until the long beans are cooked *al dente*. Turn into a bowl and serve.

VEGETABLE CURRY (CV)
GAENG PA JAY

2 tbsp vegetable oil

1 tbsp red curry paste (page 89)

1 oz/30 g krachai, peeled and cut into fine matchsticks

16 fl oz/500 ml/2 cups vegetable stock

2 oz/60 g/½ cup long beans, cut into 1 inch/2.5 cm pieces

2 oz/60 g/½ cup carrots, cut into fine matchsticks

2 oz/60 g/½ cup baby sweetcorn, roughly chopped if large

3 kaffir lime leaves, roughly chopped

2 large fresh red or green chilies, roughly chopped

2 tbsp light soy sauce

1 tsp sugar

½ tsp salt

4 small round green aubergines/eggplants (page 61), quartered

10 fresh sweet basil leaves

In a saucepan, heat the oil and quickly stir in the curry paste. Add the krachai and the vegetable stock and briefly stir, then add all the remaining ingredients except the basil. Stir well. Add the basil leaves, stir once, turn into a bowl and serve.

Top left: Steamed Mussels with Krachai (*Hoy Op Krachai*), with hot and sweet nut sauce.
Below right: Squid Stuffed with Pork and Galangal (*Pla Muk Songkla*).

FRIED FISH WITH TURMERIC (F)

PLA TOD KHAMIN

1 medium-size firm-fleshed fish (bream or sea bass would do), cleaned

1 tbsp roughly chopped turmeric

2 tsp dried white peppercorns

1 tbsp roughly chopped garlic

1 tbsp roughly chopped shallots

2 tbsp fish sauce

1 tsp sugar

vegetable oil for frying

fresh coriander leaves/cilantro, to garnish

Cut the fish into 2 inch/5 cm pieces and put in a bowl. In a mortar, pound together the turmeric, peppercorns, garlic and shallots to form a paste. Spread the paste over the fish and stir to coat well. Pour in the fish sauce and sugar and stir well to mix.

Heat about ¼ inch/5 mm of oil in a frying pan. Fry the coated fish pieces until they are crispy all over. Drain, arrange on a serving dish and garnish with coriander.

SOUTHERN CHICKEN CURRY (C)

GAI KOLAE

Kolae are southern fishing boats, usually decorated with intricate hand-painted designs – though why the Thai name for this dish should be *Kolae* chicken is unclear. None of my southern friends could offer an explanation, though one thought that the bright colour of the curry might suggest the brightly coloured vessels.

The curry:

4 tbsp vegetable oil

1 large garlic clove, finely chopped

1 chicken, weighing 3–4 lbs/1.35–1.8 kg, roughly chopped into 10–12 large pieces with skin and bones

16 fl oz/480 ml/2 cups coconut cream (page 178)

8 fl oz/240 ml/1 cup chicken stock

4 tbsp fish sauce

2 tbsp sugar

4 tbsp lime juice

10 small fresh red and green chilies/*prik kee noo*, to garnish

The paste:

5 large dried red chilies/*prik haeng*, seeded and soaked in water for 5 minutes

½ tsp salt

1 tsp roughly chopped fresh turmeric

½ tsp coriander seeds

½ tsp cumin seeds

1 tsp dried shrimp paste

To make the paste, place each ingredient in a mortar in turn and pound together to form a paste. (You should need all this paste for the following curry, but were you to make in excess of your immediate needs, the paste could be stored in a sealed container and kept in the refrigerator for a month.)

In a wok or frying pan, heat the oil and fry the garlic until golden brown. Add the chicken and fry until golden. Remove from the oil, drain and set aside.

Pour the oil from the wok into a large saucepan, heat and add the prepared paste, stirring until it begins to blend. Add half the coconut cream and stir well, then add the reserved chicken and mix well. Add the stock, stirring well. Add the second half of the coconut cream and stir; add the fish sauce and stir; add the sugar and lime juice and stir well, bringing the liquid to the boil. Lower the heat and simmer for 15 minutes.

Turn into a bowl and scatter the whole chilies on the surface. Serve immediately.

CURRIED PRAWNS/SHRIMP WITH TURMERIC (C)
GAENG LUANG

16 fl oz/500 ml/2 cups chicken stock
8 oz/240 g large raw prawns/shrimp, peeled and de-veined
6oz/180 g/1 cup bamboo shoots, roughly chopped
3 tbsp fish sauce
1 tbsp tamarind water (page 142)
1 tbsp sugar
The curry paste:
5 small dried chilies
1 tbsp finely chopped shallots
2 tbsp finely chopped garlic
1 tbsp roughly chopped turmeric
1 tbsp dried shrimp paste
½ tsp salt

First make the curry paste. Place the chilies in a mortar and pound well. Add the remaining ingredients in turn, pounding well to form a paste.

In a saucepan, heat the chicken stock, stir in 2 tablespoons of the curry paste (any extra paste can be kept in a sealed container in a refrigerator for 1 month) and bring to the boil. Add the prawns, bamboo shoots and the remaining ingredients. Return to the boil and simmer for 3 minutes. Turn into a bowl and serve.

SPIT ROASTED CHICKEN WITH TURMERIC (F)
GAI OP KHAMIN

Ideally, the chicken should be cooked on a rotary spit to let all the excess fat drain away. If this isn't possible, roast the chicken on a rack over a roasting pan in a preheated oven (375°F/190°C/gas mark 5), turning and pricking the flesh from time to time.

2 tbsp finely chopped garlic
1 tsp dried white peppercorns
1 tbsp roughly chopped coriander root
1 medium-size chicken, weighing about 3–3½ lb/1.35–1.6 kg
1 tsp salt
1 tsp turmeric powder
The sauce:
6 tbsp rice vinegar
4 tbsp sugar
½ tsp salt
2 garlic cloves, finely chopped
4 small fresh red chilies, finely chopped

Preheat the oven to 375°F/190°C/gas mark 5.

In a mortar, pound the garlic, peppercorns and coriander root together to form a paste. Smear this evenly over the chicken and sprinkle with the salt and turmeric powder.

Roast the chicken for 20 minutes per 1 lb/480 g plus 20 minutes.

Meanwhile, make the sauce. In a small saucepan, heat the vinegar, add the sugar and stir until it dissolves. Add the salt and simmer, stirring, until the liquid begins to reduce and thicken. Add the garlic and chilies. Stir well, then pour into a bowl. Serve hot, with the chicken.

COOKING FRUITS
PONRAMI

Thailand abounds in delicious fruits, both temperate from the north, and the more famous exotic tropical varieties which we now export around the world. This section is not an attempt to introduce all these fruits but only those which are cooked much as one would a vegetable.

Pineapple *Sapparot*
Young pineapple shoots can be used in curries in the same way as bamboo shoots and palm hearts, though they are unlikely to be obtainable outside pineapple-growing regions. The Thai pineapple is probably the world's sweetest; if you cannot get the real thing you should try to get the juiciest pineapple available in order to replicate the taste. Of course we all use canned pineapple in an emergency, but because the texture is soft and the syrupy sweetness cloying it is always better to try to get fresh pineapple, whatever the country of origin.

Papaya *Malako*
Thai papaya can be small and round or long and oval like a giant club, and it is probably the latter that is most commonly found in the West. We use green papaya as a vegetable; the ripe fruit is too soft except for eating raw. For Thai recipes you will have to hunt around for the unripened fruit, which is hard and green, unlike the ripened one with skins which have turned orange.

Pomelo *Som Or*
Not unlike a large, hard grapefruit, with a thicker rind and a less juicy flesh, pomelo can be pink or greeny-white. Because of their firmness and the way they separate easily, pomelo segments make an excellent cooking ingredient, though the softer grapefruit would make a reasonable substitute. The pomelo is sometimes known as a shaddock after the sea-captain who transported the fruit from South East Asia to the West Indies.

◀
Spirit houses stand above the waters, little homes to appease the spirit whose waters the fishermen are using.

▶
Cooking Fruits (*Ponrami*)
Top: Bananas (*Kluay*); Pineapple (*Sapparot*).
Centre: Mango (*Mamuang*).
Bottom: Pomelo (*Som Or*); Lychee (*Leenchee*); Papaya (*Malako*).

Lychee *Leenchee*

The lychee is well known all over the world; it survives the canning process well and is the staple dessert of many oriental restaurants. The fresh fruit grows in clusters, each one with a brittle, bumpy, rose-coloured shell. This is broken away to reveal the opal-white juicy flesh that surrounds a shiny brown nut. Provided you drain away as much of the syrup as possible, the canned lychee makes a perfectly reasonable ingredient for cooking.

Mango *Mamuang*

Devotees of the mango wax eloquent about its qualities and there is no doubt that those grown in Thailand are among the sweetest you can get. This is the result of hundreds of years of careful cultivation, which have bred out of the plant its natural and unpleasant turpentine flavour, leaving only a hint of sourness that adds an edge to the otherwise sickly sweetness. The only problem newcomers have with the fruit is how to select the best and how to prepare it once the choice is made. As for the latter, it has been suggested that the best solution is to do it in your bath tub as you can get very messy if you are not careful! The compromise solution is to peel it carefully beside a running cold tap so that you can rinse it and yourself as you go along. You will need a very sharp knife. Once peeled, you should slice the flesh away from the large flat stone/pit in the centre.

Thais eat both the fully ripened, yellow-orange mangoes and the unripe green mango, which is similar to a slightly harder Granny Smith apple. Selection is a problem – we go by shape, having a whole set of pointers to help us. For example, the *mamuang lat*, the rhino mango, so called because it has a little bump on its surface not unlike a rhino horn, is thought to be among the best of the unripened varieties, whereas the *mamuang ok rong*, a ripe mango with a cleft like a woman's cleavage, is thought to be the sweetest. I hesitate to try

and teach anyone all these signs that are part of the knowledge Thai children acquire unthinkingly as they grow. However, it need not be too much of a problem, as exported sweet mangoes have usually been carefully selected before shipping and ought to be of the best quality. For cooking purposes you need to find either the unripened green mango or, better still, the wild 'cooking' mango which remains green and sour when fully mature. The latter are found all year round, so you may get them in specialist shops at any time.

Banana *Kluay*

Although there are twenty-eight varieties of edible banana in Thailand, ranging from the large savory plantain to the tiny sweet dwarf banana, the use of the fruit is usually limited to the making of desserts. The Laotians and the Vietnamese do make a savoury vegetable dish using tiny immature bananas, but in Thailand such use of bananas is confined to those areas where the influence of those cuisines is strongest, most noticeably the North East. For the rest of the country, even the unsweet plantain banana is transformed into a dessert by frying thin slices and then sugaring them. In the only savoury version, plantain is fried and lightly salted to be eaten like crisps or chips as a snack. It is, however, the familiar common banana, long yellow and sweet, that most concerns us and that is easily available everywhere.

RECIPES
WITH COOKING FRUITS

PINEAPPLE FRIED WITH GINGER (FV)
PAD KING SAPPAROT

5 large dried black fungus mushrooms
2 tbsp vegetable oil
2 garlic cloves, finely chopped
1 medium-size onion, roughly chopped
6 oz/180 g/1¼ cups pineapple chunks
2 inch/5 cm piece of fresh ginger, peeled and cut into fine matchsticks
2 tbsp light soy sauce
2 tbsp vegetable stock
2 spring onions/scallions, chopped into 1 inch/2.5 cm pieces
1 long fresh red chili/*prik chee faa*, cut diagonally into fine ovals
½ tsp sugar
pinch of salt
black pepper to taste

Soak the mushrooms in cold water for 10 minutes.

In a wok or frying pan, heat the oil and fry the garlic until golden brown. Add the mushrooms and stir well. Stirring constantly, add all remaining ingredients in turn. As soon as the pepper is stirred in, turn on to a dish and serve.

RAW PAPAYA SALAD (Y)
SOMTAM

4 oz/120 g fresh unripened papaya, peeled and seeded
2 small garlic cloves, peeled
1 tbsp roasted peanuts
3 small fresh red or green chilies
1 oz/30 g/⅓ cup long beans, chopped into 1 inch/2.5 cm pieces
2 tbsp fish sauce
2 tbsp lime juice
1 tbsp sugar
1 medium-size tomato, sliced into rounds
lettuce leaves, to serve

Sliver the papaya into matchstick-like pieces using a grater or a knife. Set aside.

In a mortar, pound together the garlic and the peanuts, then pound in the chilies. Add the long bean and pound until broken up, then add the papaya slivers and pound lightly, turning the mixture with a spoon held in the other hand so that the fruit is impregnated with all the ingredients. Pour in the fish sauce, lime juice and sugar and stir well to mix thoroughly. Add the tomatoes and briefly pound before mixing.

Arrange the lettuce leaves on a platter and place the pounded salad at the centre. Use the lettuce leaves as scoops to eat the salad.

Top left: Waterchestnuts with Bandan Leaf and Coconut Cream (*Tako Hel*). Top right: Taro with Palm Sugar and Coconut Milk (*Pua Gaeng Buad*). Bottom left: Bananas in Coconut Milk (*Kluay Bua Chee*). Bottom centre and right: Moong Bean Custard (*Kanom Maw Gaeng*) – the centre custard is decorated with lotus seeds.

BANANAS IN COCONUT MILK (L)

KLUAY BUA CHEE

12 fl oz/360 ml/1½ cups coconut milk (page 178)

2 tbsp sugar

½ tsp salt

2 long bananas, peeled, cut in half lengthways and then quartered crossways to make 16 pieces in all

In a saucepan, heat the coconut milk and add the sugar and salt. Bring to the boil, stirring until dissolved. Add the banana pieces. Return to the boil and simmer for 3 minutes.

Remove from the heat and leave for a few moments, then serve warm. You can reheat this or serve any leftovers cold from the refrigerator.

HOT AND SOUR POMELO SALAD (Y)

YAM SOM OH

2 tbsp vegetable oil

1 oz/30 g garlic, sliced into fine rounds

1 oz/30 g shallots, sliced into fine ovals

3 tbsp coconut milk (page 178)

1 tbsp Grilled Chili Oil/*Nam Prik Pow* (page 84)

6 oz/180 g cooked boneless chicken, pulled into fine shreds

2 tbsp fish sauce

2 tbsp lime juice

1 tbsp sugar

10 oz/300 g/1½–2 cups fresh pomelo segments, or use large grapefruit segments

2 tbsp ground roasted peanuts

4 small fresh red or green chilies, finely chopped

fresh coriander leaves/cilantro, to garnish

In a wok or frying pan, heat the oil and fry the garlic until crispy; remove with a slotted spoon and set aside. Fry the shallots until crispy; remove and set aside.

In a large saucepan, heat the coconut milk and stir in the *Nam Prik Pow*, mixing well. As it begins to reduce and thicken, add the shredded chicken and stir. Add the fish sauce, lime juice and sugar. Stir well and remove from the heat.

Add the pomelo, peanuts, fresh chilies and the reserved crispy garlic and shallots. Toss well. Turn on to a serving dish, garnish with coriander leaves and serve.

PRAWN/SHRIMP AND LYCHEE SPRING ROLL (H)
— PO PIA HAT YAI —

12 spring roll sheets, each 4 inches/10 cm square

6 large raw prawns/shrimp, peeled but leaving the tail on, de-veined and sliced in half lengthways

6 large peeled lychees (fresh or canned), finely chopped

salt and ground black pepper

1 egg, whisked

vegetable oil for deep frying

The sauce:

6 tbsp rice vinegar

4 tbsp sugar

½ tsp salt

1 tbsp ground roasted peanuts

4 small fresh red or green chilies, finely chopped

Take one spring roll sheet and fold over one corner towards the centre. Lay a half prawn on the sheet with its tail hanging over the folded edge. Lay half of one chopped lychee along the length of the prawn and sprinkle with salt and pepper. Roll up the spring roll sheet from one side of the prawn to the other so that you are left with a cylinder like a fat cigarette with the tail protruding from one end. Seal the spring roll with whisked egg. Repeat the process to make the remaining spring rolls. Set aside.

To make the sauce, in a small saucepan, heat the vinegar and stir in the sugar until dissolved. Stir in the salt, nuts and chilies. Stir well and turn into a bowl.

Heat a pan of oil for deep frying to 400°F/200°C. Deep fry the spring rolls until they are golden brown all over. Drain on paper towels and serve hot, with the sauce.

HOT AND SOUR GRILLED PORK WITH GREEN MANGO (Y)
— MOO KOH YOR —

2 oz/60 g unripened green mango flesh (unpeeled)

6 oz/180 g pork fillet/tenderloin

2 tbsp fish sauce

2 tbsp lemon juice

1 tsp sugar

½ tsp chili powder

2 shallots, finely chopped

2 kaffir lime leaves, rolled up into a cigarette shape and finely sliced across

Sliver the mango into matchstick-like pieces using a grater or a knife. Set aside.

Preheat the grill/broiler. Place the whole pork fillet under the hot grill and cook, turning once, until golden brown and cooked through. Slice finely, reserving any juices.

Put the pork and its juices into a wok or frying pan, and heat as you add the remaining ingredients in turn, stirring between each. After a final stir, turn on to a plate and serve.

COCONUT
MAPROW

While the coconut palm is found mainly in coastal regions, the myriad products obtained from it are an essential part of Thai life all over the country. From furniture to musical instruments, from palm wine to soap, this remarkable tree is probably the single most useful plant in the kingdom. The fruit of the palm, the coconut, is used in cooking at all stages of its development.

The young unopened leaves, the core at the top of the stem (sometimes called 'palm heart' or 'heart of palm') can be eaten. Although you are unlikely to find fresh palm hearts outside coconut-growing regions, the canned variety can be used exactly like bamboo shoots in the recipes on pages 120–1.

When first grown to full size, the young green coconut contains a refreshing clear liquid that should not be confused with coconut cream or milk; the latter two are produced from the hardened nut. If the coconut is left to ripen on the tree this clear liquid gradually forms into the white coconut meat. When it is still soft, it is deliciously sweet and is much used in Thai curries and desserts. If allowed to ripen fully, this meat hardens into the white nut more familiar in the West. It is from this that coconut cream and milk are produced.

Coconut Cream and Milk

Coconut cream and its thinner form, coconut milk, are available from a number of sources. Authentically, of course, they are made from fresh mature coconuts, but there are a number of short cuts. You can buy blocks of coconut, which are not unlike blocks of white wax; these are heated according to the instructions on the packet and dissolve into a cream. You can also buy powdered coconut milk, which again includes instructions on adding water to produce the desired liquid mixture. I cannot really recommend either of these methods, as the manufacturers tend to adulterate the coconut with flour which produces a somewhat stale flavour. By far the best short cut is to use cans of coconut milk, which are easily available and made from fresh mature coconuts. Some brands do add a little flour but not enough to spoil the flavour.

◀
Grating coconut, first part of the process of making coconut cream.

▶
Against a background of lotus leaves:
Top: Young coconut (the green outer shell cut away in traditional style), filled with fresh coconut juice or water.
Centre left: Mature coconut filled with desiccated coconut.
Centre right: Mature coconut showing the inner 'meat' which is used to make coconut cream and milk.
Bottom: Mature coconut into which the finished milk has been poured.

Once the can is opened, you have only to let the heavier cream settle to the bottom to be able to pour off the thinner milk, allowing you to use whichever is required. In the great majority of cases, it will simply suffice for you to shake the can before opening and use the mixed liquid.

If you prefer to make your own unadulterated cream and milk, you can do so by using fresh mature coconuts, or unsweetened desiccated coconuts, using the following methods:

Break open a fresh mature coconut, one with the hard brown outer shell, and grate the inner 'meat'. Place the meat in a large bowl and pour over warm water (just hot enough for you to comfortably place your hand in it) in the following proportions: for every 8 oz/ 240 g of coconut there should be 16 fl oz/500 ml/ 2 cups of warm water. You should then stir up the meat in the water for 5 seconds. Place a sieve lined with muslin/cheesecloth over a second bowl. Pour in the liquid and the meat and squeeze until all the liquid is forced out and into the bowl. Because the fresh meat contains juice, this, plus the water, should produce about 24 fl oz/750 ml/3 cups of coconut cream. You should now put the squeezed coconut meat back into the first bowl, pour over it a second 16 fl oz/500 ml/2 cups of warm water and leave this to soak for 10 minutes. After soaking, repeat the sieving and squeezing process, which should produce about 16 fl oz/500 ml/2 cups of thinner coconut milk.

If you are using unsweetened desiccated coconut, follow the same procedure but with 8 oz/240 g of unsweetened desiccated coconut mixed with 20 fl oz/625 ml/2½ cups of warm water. Leave to soak for 10 minutes, then sieve and squeeze to produce approximately 16 fl oz/ 500 ml/2 cups of a liquid which will be halfway between cream and milk. You could reduce the water if you feel you really need to thicken this and make it creamier, but in my experience it will pass for cream in most recipes.

Coconut cream and milk can be frozen and stored in a deep freezer, otherwise store in a refrigerator but use within two days.

RECIPES
WITH COCONUT

GREEN BEEF CURRY WITH YOUNG COCONUT (C)
GAENG KIOW WAN MA PROW

2 tbsp vegetable oil
2 garlic cloves, finely chopped
8 oz/240 g tender boneless beef steak, finely sliced, retaining fat
8 fl oz/240 ml/1 cup coconut cream (page 178)
8 fl oz/240 ml/1 cup beef stock
4 oz/120 g young fresh coconut meat, in rough shavings
2 large fresh red chilies, sliced diagonally into fine ovals
2 tbsp fish sauce
1 tsp sugar
20 fresh sweet basil leaves
The green curry paste:
2 long fresh green chilies/*prik chee faa*, chopped
10 small fresh green chilies, chopped
1 tbsp chopped tender lemon grass
3 shallots, chopped
2 tbsp chopped garlic
1 inch/2.5 cm piece of galangal, peeled and chopped
3 coriander roots, chopped
1 tsp ground coriander
½ tsp ground cumin
½ tsp ground white pepper
1 tsp chopped kaffir lime rind
2 tsp dried shrimp paste
1 tsp salt

For the curry paste: in a mortar, pound the ingredients together, adding them in turn, to form a smooth paste. Set aside. Any unused paste may be stored in a sealed container in a refrigerator for up to 1 month.

In a large saucepan, heat the oil and fry the garlic until golden brown. Stir in 1 tablespoon of the curry paste, mixing well. Add the beef and stir-fry until just cooked through. Add the coconut cream and stir well, bringing to the boil. Add the stock. Return to the boil, stirring constantly. Simmer, stirring in all the remaining ingredients except the basil. Stir in the basil leaves just before pouring into a bowl to serve.

WATERCHESTNUTS WITH BANDAN LEAF AND COCONUT CREAM (K)
TAKO HEL

To make this recipe, you must find bandan leaf in an oriental store. You will need to buy an entire cut plant, which will have about ten leaves. These should be placed in a mortar and thoroughly pounded to extract their juice. The yield should be about 4 fl oz/120 ml/½ cup of liquid.

10 jasmin flowers or 4 drops of concentrated flower essence such as rose water
1¼ pints/720 ml/3 cups water
8 oz/240 g/2 cups rice flour
4 fl oz/120 ml/½ cup bandan juice
8 oz/240 g/1 cup waterchestnuts, finely diced
8 oz/240 g/1¼ cups sugar
The coconut cream:
4 oz/120 g/1 cup rice flour
8 fl oz/240 ml/1 cup coconut cream (page 178)
¼ tsp salt

Steep the jasmin flowers in the water for 1 hour to perfume it, and strain, or stir the flower essence into the water. Heat the perfumed water in a large saucepan. Add the rice flour, bandan juice, waterchestnuts and sugar and cook, stirring constantly, until the mixture thickens. Turn into small serving bowls and set aside while you prepare the coconut cream.

In a saucepan, gently heat all the ingredients, stirring until the mixture thickens. Pour a little over each bowl and serve.

CRAB AND COCONUT CAKES WITH PLUM SAUCE (H)
— TOD MAN POO —

Preserved plums are sold in bottles in Chinese shops.

8 oz/240 g fresh crab meat
1 oz/30 g/⅓ cup unsweetened desiccated/ dried shredded coconut
1 egg
2 garlic cloves, finely chopped
1 tbsp fish sauce
1 tbsp oyster sauce
sprinkling of ground white pepper
fine dry white breadcrumbs, to coat
vegetable oil for deep frying
The plum sauce:
1 preserved plum
2 small fresh red or green chilies, finely chopped
6 tbsp rice vinegar
4 tbsp sugar

First make the sauce. Using a fork, scrape the plum flesh from the stone/pit. In a saucepan, heat the vinegar and dissolve the sugar. Stir in the plum flesh. Simmer until a thin syrup begins to form, then remove from the heat. Stir in the chilies. Pour into a bowl and set aside.

In a mixing bowl, stir together the crab, coconut, egg, garlic, sauces and pepper. Knead with your fingers and form into small patties. Roll in the breadcrumbs until well coated.

Heat a pan of oil for deep frying to 400°F/200°C. Deep fry the patties until golden brown all over. Drain on paper towels and serve immediately, with the plum sauce.

PRAWN/SHRIMP SATAY AMANPURI (H)
— GUNG SATAY —

1 tsp coriander seeds
1 tsp cumin seeds
12 large raw prawns/shrimp, peeled but leaving the tails on
2 tbsp light soy sauce
1 tsp salt
4 tbsp vegetable oil
1 tbsp curry powder
1 tbsp ground turmeric
4 fl oz/120 ml/½ cup coconut milk (page 178)
3 tbsp sugar
The peanut sauce:
2 tbsp vegetable oil
3 garlic cloves, finely chopped
1 tbsp red curry paste (page 89)
4 fl oz/120 ml/½ cup coconut milk (page 178)
8 fl oz/240 ml/1 cup chicken stock
1 tbsp sugar
1 tbsp salt
1 tbsp lemon juice
4 tbsp crushed roasted peanuts
4 tbsp dried breadcrumbs

In a small saucepan, fry the coriander and cumin seeds for 5 minutes, stirring to ensure that they do not burn. Transfer them to a mortar and pound to a fine powder.

Put the prawns in a bowl and add all the remaining ingredients, including the ground coriander and cumin. Stir well and leave to marinate for at least 8 hours.

Meanwhile, make the peanut sauce. In a frying pan, heat the oil and fry the garlic until golden brown. Mix in the curry paste and cook for a few seconds. Add the coconut milk, mix and cook for a few seconds. Add the stock, sugar, salt and lemon juice and stir to blend. Cook for 1 minute, stirring constantly, then add the ground peanuts and breadcrumbs and blend thoroughly. Pour into a bowl and set aside.

Preheat the grill/broiler. Thread each prawn, tail first, on to an 8 inch/20 cm wooden satay stick. Place under the grill and cook the satays until the prawns are pink and opaque, about 6–8 minutes, turning to make sure they are browned on both sides. Serve with the peanut sauce and a fresh pickle/*adjahd* (page 26).

CARAMELIZED COCONUT (K)
NAA GRACHEE

In Thailand we would use jasmin flowers to scent the water for this dish, but a flower essence can be substituted.

5 jasmin flowers or 2 drops of concentrated flower essence such as rose water
8 fl oz/240 ml/1 cup water
3 tbsp palm sugar (page 184)
8 oz/240 g/2⅓ cups unsweetened desiccated/dried shredded coconut
steamed sticky rice (page 24), to serve

Steep the jasmin flowers in the water for 1 hour to perfume it, and strain, or stir the flower essence into the water. Put the scented water into a saucepan on a low heat. Add the palm sugar and slowly dissolve it, stirring constantly. As it dissolves, stir in the coconut and continue stirring and heating gently until a caramel sauce is formed. Do not let it thicken to a point where it will harden.

Remove from the heat while still liquid. Allow to cool, then pour over mounds of sticky rice.

COCONUT CUSTARD (K)
SANG KIAA

In Thailand we use duck eggs for this recipe, which are big and give a rich dark colour to the custard, but here I am using ordinary hen's eggs.

8 fl oz/240 ml/1 cup coconut milk (page 178)
3 tbsp/palm sugar (page 184)
4 hen's eggs (UK size 2. US extra large)
steamed sticky rice (page 24), to serve

In a large bowl, mix the coconut milk with the palm sugar, stirring until it has dissolved. Beat in the eggs, mixing well. Pour into a metal baking dish, about 2 inches/5 cm deep.

Bring water to the boil in the bottom part of a steamer. Set the dish in the top part of a steamer, cover and steam for 25–30 minutes or until the tines of a fork inserted into the custard come out clean. Leave to cool.

Place a portion of sticky rice on each plate and cover with thin scoops of custard, spooned out of the baking dish.

▶

Mysteriously beautiful, the Wat Yala temple inside an underground cavern in southern Thailand.

184 Palm sugar is produced from the sap of the coconut palm. Several varieties of palm can provide suitable sap but the commonest are the coconut palm and the sugar palm, each of which gives a slightly different flavoured sugar, though the standard commercial product, sold in cans or cakes, has a fairly uniform taste. The unique quality of palm sugar is its deep caramel flavour, quite different from ordinary cane sugar.

If coconut sap is left to ferment for just a day you get palm wine or palm toddy, a highly alcoholic beverage. If the sap is boiled down until it crystallizes, you get a coarse sticky sugar. The deep flavour of palm sugar adds a distinctive edge to Thai confections, but it is also used to add another dimension to savoury dishes such as curries.

If you only plan to use a little at a time you should try to buy well-compressed cakes of palm sugar, as these will keep for a long time in a well-sealed jar. The best is soft brown in colour and has a distinctive toffee-like aroma. You should be able to find it without difficulty in oriental stores.

MOONG BEAN CUSTARD (K)
KANOM MAW GAENG

14 oz/420 g/2 cups dried moong beans (page 145)

16 fl oz/500 ml/2 cups coconut cream (page 178)

3 eggs, lightly beaten

3 tbsp palm sugar

2 tbsp vegetable oil

4 shallots, finely sliced

Rinse the moong beans in cold water. Put them in a saucepan and cover with about 2 inches/5 cm of water. Bring to the boil then simmer gently for 30–45 minutes or until the beans are completely soft.

Drain off any excess water and mash the beans to a smooth paste. Stir in the coconut cream, eggs, and palm sugar. Pour the mixture into a shallow, greased pan, about 9 x 9 x 2 inches/23 x 23 x 5 cm.

Preheat the oven to 350°F/180°C/gas mark 4. Bake the custard for about 1 hour or until golden brown on top and quite firm when pressed lightly.

While the custard is baking, heat the oil in a small wok or frying pan and fry the shallots until dark golden brown. Drain on paper towels and set aside.

About 10 minutes before you take the custard from the oven, preheat the grill/broiler.

When the custard is baked, put it under the grill to crisp the top – about 5 minutes. Leave to cool. Before serving, sprinkle the fried shallots over the top and cut into small squares (about 2 inch/5 cm).

VEGETARIAN CRISPY NOODLES (FV)

MEE KROP

Although laborious to make, this rather sweet dish is an excellent accompaniment to curries.

vegetable oil for deep frying

4 oz/120 g *sen mee* noodles, soaked and drained

The sauce:

2 tbsp vegetable oil

4 oz/120 g ready-fried beancurd, cut into thin strips

2 garlic cloves, finely chopped

2 small shallots, finely chopped

1 tbsp light soy sauce

½ tsp salt

2 tbsp palm sugar

4 tbsp vegetable stock

3 tbsp lemon juice

½ tsp chili powder

To garnish:

2 tbsp vegetable oil

1 egg, lightly beaten with 1 tbsp cold water

1 oz/30 g/⅓ cup beansprouts

1 spring onion/scallion, cut into 1 inch/2.5 cm slivers

1 medium-size fresh red chili, seeded and slivered lengthways

1 whole head of pickled garlic/*kratiam dong* (page 98), sliced across the bulb to make flower-shaped sections.

Heat a pan of oil for deep frying to 400°F/200°C. Deep fry the noodles until golden brown and crispy. Drain on paper towels and set aside.

For the sauce, heat the oil in a wok or frying pan and fry the beancurd until crisp. Remove and set aside. Add the garlic to the pan and fry until golden brown; drain and set aside. Add the shallots to the pan and fry until golden brown. Stir in the soy sauce, salt, palm sugar, stock and lemon juice. Cook, stirring, until the mixture begins to caramelize. Add the chili powder and the reserved beancurd and garlic and stir until they have soaked up some of the liquid. Remove from the heat and set aside.

In a separate wok or frying pan, heat the oil for the garnish and drip in the egg mixture to make little scraps of fried egg. Drain and set aside.

Return the pan of sauce to the heat and crumble in the crispy noodles, mixing gently and briefly. Turn on to a serving dish and sprinkle with the beansprouts, spring onion, fried egg scraps, chili and pickled garlic 'flowers'. Serve immediately.

EGGS WITH PALM SUGAR (F)

KAI LOOK KOEI

vegetable oil for deep frying + 2 tbsp

6 eggs, hard-boiled and shelled

1 small onion, finely sliced

4 tbsp fish sauce

2 tbsp palm sugar

½ tsp pounded dried red chili

Heat a pan of oil for deep frying to 400°F/200°C. Lower in the eggs and fry gently, carefully turning, until they are an even light golden brown. Remove, drain on paper towels and cut in half lengthways. Arrange on a serving dish and set aside.

In a wok or frying pan, heat the 2 tablespoons of oil and fry the onion until crisp and golden brown. Remove with a slotted spoon, drain and set aside. Turn down the heat and add the fish sauce, palm sugar and chili to the oil, stirring until the sugar dissolves. Cook for a further minute or until the mixture begins to thicken, then stir in the reserved onions. Continue cooking briefly, stirring until well mixed, then pour over the eggs and serve.

TARO WITH PALM SUGAR AND COCONUT MILK (L)

PUA GAENG BUAD

Despite its forbidding appearance – a large oval tuber with brown hairy skin – the taro is very similar to a potato. When peeled, the taro has white to purplish flesh which must be cooked to detoxify the calcium oxalate it contains. That done, the taro comes into its own, for while it is bland, like a potato, the taro is much smoother and creamier.

1 whole taro, (approx 10 oz/300 ml) peeled and roughly cut into 1 inch/2.5 cm cubes
2 tsp salt
16 fl oz/500 ml/2 cups coconut milk (page 178)
3 tbsp palm sugar
8 fl oz/240 ml/1 cup coconut cream (page 178)

Put the taro cubes in a bowl of cold water, add the salt and leave to soak for 30 minutes. Drain.

In a saucepan, heat the coconut milk, add the taro cubes and bring to the boil. Add the palm sugar and stir until it dissolves. Stir in the coconut cream. Return to the boil, then immediately remove from the heat and serve warm.

DUMPLINGS WITH PALM SUGAR SAUCE (K)

KANOM TOM DAENG

8 oz/240 g/2 cups glutinous rice flour
12 fl oz/360 ml/1½ cups water
3 tbsp palm sugar
6 oz/180 g/2 cups unsweetened desiccated/dried shredded coconut

Place the flour in a bowl and add the water drop by drop, mixing to make a malleable dough. Roll the dough into little balls about ½ inch/1.25 cm diameter. Press the balls flat to make 1 inch/2.5 cm patties. Set aside.

In a saucepan, mix together the palm sugar and coconut and slowly heat, stirring constantly to make a caramel syrup.

Remove from the heat and set aside.

Bring a pan of water to the boil. Add the patties. When they rise to the surface as dumplings, remove and drain on paper towels. Add them to the saucepan with the syrup. Mix well and serve.

SWEET AND HOT FISH SAUCE (D)

NAM PLOW WAN

This is a basic sauce used as an accompaniment to grilled fish and seafood. In Thailand it is thought to be especially good with catfish and lobster.

2 tbsp vegetable oil
2 dried chilies, cut into thin rings
2 garlic cloves, cut into fine ovals
2 small shallots, cut into fine ovals
2 tbsp palm sugar
3 tbsp fish sauce
1 tbsp tamarind water (page 142)

Heat the oil in a small wok or frying pan and fry the chilies until crispy. Remove with a slotted spoon, drain on paper towels and set aside. Fry the garlic until crispy; remove, drain and set aside. Fry the shallots until crispy; remove, drain and set aside.

In a saucepan over a low heat, melt the palm sugar. Add the fish sauce and stir well. Add the tamarind juice and cook, stirring, until a thin syrup begins to form. Stir in the reserved crispy chilies, garlic and shallots. Stir well, then turn into a bowl for serving. Thais would always serve a bunch of fresh coriander/cilantro alongside as a balancing accompaniment.

▶

Palm Sugar (*Nam Tan Peep*)

SOURCE LIST FOR THAI INGREDIENTS

IN THE UNITED STATES:

New York:
Chinese-American Trading Co.
91 Mulberry Street
New York, NY 100013
212–267–5224

9–8 PM
Curry paste and coconut milk

California:
The Bangkok Market, Inc.
4804–6 Melrose Ave.
Los Angeles, CA 90029
213–662–7990

9–9 PM

For Wholesale/Mail Order:
3718 E. 26th St.
Vernon, CA 90023
213–264–4898

Catalog Available
A large array of fresh and dried
Thai ingredients.

Texas:
Asian Grocery
9191 Forest Lane #3
Dallas, TX 75243
214–235–3038

10–7 PM
A large array of fresh and dried
Thai ingredients.

Oregon:
Anzen Japanese Foods and Imports
736 Martin Luther King Jr. Blvd.
Portland, OR 97232
503–233–5111

9–6.30 PM M-Sat
12–5 PM Sun.

Price Sheet Available
A large array of fresh and dried
Thai ingredients.

Washington:
Uwajimaya
519 6th avenue South
Seattle, WA 98104
206–624–6248

9–8 PM
Catalog Available
A large array of fresh and dried
Thai ingredients.

IN THE UK:

As most British towns have at least
one Chinese store, and usually an
Indian, Pakistani or Bangladeshi
store as well, finding all but the
most obscure ingredients in this
book should not be a problem.
Many supermarket chains now
stock some Thai products. The
following are Thai shops which sell
specifically Thai goods:

London:
Sri Thai
56 Shepherd's Bush Road
London W6
Tel: 071 602 0621

Talad Thai
320 Upper Richmond Road
Putney
London SW15
Tel: 081 789 8084

Tawana
18–20 Chepstow Road
London W2
Tel: 071 221 6316

Manchester:
Kim Thai Supermarket
46 George Street
Manchester M1 4HF
Tel: 061 228 6263